Attention Deficit/ Hyperactivity Disorder

A

Attention Deficit/ Hyperactivity Disorder

Other books in the At Issue series:

Attention Deficit/ Hyperactivity Disorder

William Dudley, *Book Editor*

Bruce Glassman, *Vice President*
Bonnie Szumski, *Publisher*
Helen Cothran, *Managing Editor*

GREENHAVEN PRESS
An imprint of Thomson Gale, a part of The Thomson Corporation

THOMSON
━━━━━✳━━━━━™
GALE

Detroit • New York • San Francisco • San Diego • New Haven, Conn.
Waterville, Maine • London • Munich

For more information, contact
Greenhaven Press
27500 Drake Rd.
Farmington Hills, MI 48331-3535
Or you can visit our Internet site at http://www.gale.com

LIBRARY OF CONGRESS CATALOGING-IN-PUBLICATION DATA

Attention deficit/hyperactivity disorder / William Dudley, book editor.
    p. cm. — (At issue)
   Includes bibliographical references and index.
   ISBN 0-7377-2258-4 (lib. : alk. paper) — ISBN 0-7377-2259-2 (pbk. : alk. paper)
    1. Attention/deficit hyperactivity disorder. I. Dudley, William. II. At issue (San Diego, Calif.)
   RJ506.H9A92 2005
   618.92'8589—dc22   2004054303

Contents

Introduction

Attention deficit disorder (ADD) and attention deficit/hyperactivity disorder (ADHD) are names given to a condition found in children and adults. The disorder is characterized by inattention, distractibility, impulsivity, and, in some cases, hyperactivity. (The condition is called hyperkinetic disorder outside the United States.) It is most often diagnosed in children, although in recent years more adults have been diagnosed and treated for ADHD.

According to the National Institute of Mental Health, one of the first descriptions of a child with ADHD comes from an 1845 poem by Heinrich Hoffman, a physician who wrote books about medicine and psychiatry, and who also wrote a series of poems about children to read to his young son. His poem "The Story of Fidgety Philip" begins:

> Let me see if Philip can
> Be a little gentleman;
> Let me see if he is able
> To sit still for once at table:
> Thus Papa bade Phil behave;
> And Mamma looked very grave.
> But fidgety Phil,
> He won't sit still;
> He wriggles,
> And giggles,
> And then, I declare,
> Swings backwards and forwards,
> And tilts up his chair,
> Just like any rocking-horse
> "Philip! I am getting cross!"

Philip's behavior, and the general symptoms of ADHD, probably appear in all children to some extent. But for some children, the inability to focus on tasks, sit still, or think before acting becomes so pronounced that it causes havoc in school and at home, and interferes with the child's development and maturity. Scientists estimate that between 3 and 9 percent of school-aged children are affected enough to be classified as having ADHD.

Despite the fact that in recent years ADHD has become the most common psychiatric diagnosis for children, controversies remain about its causes, treatment, and even its status as a disease. While ADHD does appear to run in families and have a genetic component, scientists have been unable to isolate or prove a genetic cause. Other theories of causation that have been proposed include nutrition, viral infections, exposure to environmental toxins, and traumatic brain injury. Scientists theorize that imbalances in neurotransmitters—the chemicals that transmit messages in the brain—lie beneath the behavioral symptoms of ADHD.

Since the 1950s ADHD has been treated with prescription drugs, the most popular of which is Ritalin, a powerful stimulant that is regulated as a controlled substance by the Drug Enforcement Administration. About 6 million children between the ages of five and eighteen, or roughly one in eight children, take Ritalin or other ADHD medications. In some cases, doctors are prescribing Ritalin to children as young as two. Advocates of these drugs say that they help at least 70 percent of people with ADHD. But many parents and others have questioned whether the health of children is being harmed in the long term by these drugs. In a few extreme cases, parents have blamed these drugs for killing their children. Since 1999 several states have passed laws barring local school officials from recommending Ritalin and other drugs to children with behaviorial problems.

Some opponents of giving drugs to children go further and question whether ADHD is a real biologically based disease. Family psychologist and parenting advice columnist John Rosemond is among those who question the very existence of ADHD. He argues that its symptoms—being impulsive, being unable to focus, and being fidgety—could describe the actions of any child at the age of two. "The typical toddler is unfocused, inattentive, and impulsive," he wrote in a 2003 column. "The pertinent question is: Do the child's parents, with a combination of powerful love and powerful discipline . . . 'cure' this anti-social state before the child's third birthday?" Rosemond and others believe that environmental factors such as lax parental discipline are the true causes of the disruptive behaviors associated with ADHD—behaviors that he says should instead be called TIP (Toddlerhood in Perpetuity).

Despite the criticisms of Rosemond and others, most scientists and medical professionals accept ADHD as a valid disorder established by years of scientific research—a position shared by the American Medical Association, American Psychological Association, American Academy of Pediatrics, and other organizations. A 2002 statement issued by seventy-five medical researchers and doctors asserted that "to publish stories that ADHD is a fictitious disorder or merely a conflict between today's Huckleberry Finns and their caregivers is tantamount to declaring the earth flat, the laws of gravity debatable, and the periodic table in chemistry a fraud." Regardless of whether the causes of ADHD stem from genetic or environmental factors, the millions of children and adults diagnosed with the disorder will continue to find their lives affected by the condition.

1

Attention Deficit/Hyperactivity Disorder Is a Serious Problem for Many Children

Vidya Bhushan Gupta

Vidya Bhushan Gupta is a doctor and pediatrics professor at the New York Medical College and the author of the book No Apologies for Ritalin.

Attention deficit/hyperactivity disorder (ADHD) is a be-havioral disorder that affects millions of children. Its symptoms include distractibility, impulsivity, and prob-lems with social behavior. While it is sometimes difficult to draw the line between abnormal and normal child be-havior, for some children their actions are problematic enough as to pose major problems for their develop-ment and maturity. ADHD can be found in all countries and among children of all social and economic classes.

Shawn

Shawn, a 6-year-old African-American child, arrives at the behavioral pediatrics clinic of a city hospital with his 55-year-old foster mother, who is a visibly harried African-American woman. The nurse cheerfully greets Shawn, but, unmindful of her greeting, he walks over to the computer at the nursing sta-tion, frantically taps its keys, and returns to pull at the stetho-

Vidya Bhushan Gupta, "A Closer Look at ADD/ADHD," *Exceptional Parent*, August 2000. Copyright © 2000 by *Exceptional Parent*. Reproduced by permission.

scope hanging around her neck. Not five seconds in the pediatrician's office, he touches the garbage can, the container for discarding used needles, and the blood pressure instrument. He then crawls under the pediatrician's chair to look into the filing cabinet. He continues in this vein despite continued requests to sit down and play with the dollhouse or to draw something. Smiling impishly—completely unaware of the havoc he is wreaking—his large eyes and cute demeanor disguise his turbulent mind.

> *His teacher repeatedly reports that Shawn does not sit quietly in the classroom, forgets instructions, disturbs other children, and constantly interrupts her.*

"He cannot stay still," his foster mother—who is actually his grandmother—says. "He is always on the go, running all over the house, turning on and off the television, opening and closing the refrigerator. He stays up 'til 11 P.M. and then doesn't fall asleep until midnight. And he even tosses and turns in his sleep. Just look at these notes from school." She pulls a wad of crumpled papers from her pocketbook. His teacher repeatedly reports that Shawn does not sit quietly in the classroom, forgets instructions, disturbs other children, and constantly interrupts her. The principal wants a doctor's note that Shawn is on a medication to calm him before he is allowed back in the classroom.

"Don't touch anything!" his foster mother constantly admonishes the boy, who continues doing exactly what he was doing.

A second case study

Melissa

Melissa, a 10-year-old Caucasian girl, is brought by her mother to the clinic because she is failing in school.

"Melissa is hyper; she acts silly to get attention, at times even by deliberately offending people. If nothing else works, she touches and pulls at them," her mother says. "She talks constantly, interrupting others, and can't wait her turn."

In school, her mother continues, although Melissa is quick

to respond, her answers are often thoughtless and wrong. "She forgets to bring homework home, and, if she does bring it, she either takes three or four hours to complete it or doesn't finish it at all. Her room is always a pigpen. I have to ask her at least ten times before she does anything," her mother continues. "No one likes her. She tries to boss other children around. When they exclude her, she throws a tantrum."

As she enters the room, Melissa rushes to give the doctor, whom she has never seen before, a warm hug. He gently disentangles himself and asks her to draw a picture of her house and the people in it, while he talks with her mother. Melissa turns immediately to the nurse, asks her name, why she is not wearing a white nurse's uniform, and "What's that thing hanging on the wall?" The nurse reminds her of the doctor's request for a picture. Melissa innocently rests her head on her closed fist and says, "I forgot." Before the nurse can reply, Melissa interrupts the doctor, "What did you ask me to draw?" Without waiting for a reply or looking at the drawing table, she asks the nurse, "Where are the crayons?" They are on the table. While drawing, she constantly interrupts the doctor with questions, saying "excuse me" each time: "Can I also draw my dog? Can I draw the sun? Is it alright to draw a bird?" She leaves the drawing twice, once to check the door when someone knocks, and once to pick up a ringing phone. She crumples three drawings before she finishes. Her final picture is chaotic, with too many people, things, and animals, each hurriedly drawn and with unnecessary shading. She asks the doctor, "Did I do good?" "Look mommy," she exclaims, "I also drew my cat. Can we go now?"

"Will you shut up!" her exasperated mother shouts.

"How was she as a baby?" the doctor asks.

"A real handful. She was a colicky baby; kept me awake at nights. And a terrible toddler, always running around, always saying 'no!'"

Healthy or sick?

Jason

Jason, a 12-year-old Hispanic child, is brought to the clinic because he is doing so poorly in school that he might be held back. The school wants to evaluate him for special education. His mother says that he is intelligent, but just does not put his mind to his work. "He's a nice kid," she says. "The teacher's too old, she doesn't know how to handle children. She wants to put everyone in special education. He's not hyper, doesn't bother anybody. He's just lazy."

His teacher, on the other hand, reports that Jason is inattentive and daydreams in class. He often looks out the window instead of at the blackboard, and has to be repeatedly reminded to pay attention. He forgets to take notes and does not follow instructions. He fidgets and squirms in his seat, his desk is messy, and his pens and pencils keep falling off. No one wants to sit next to him.

In the doctor's office, Jason sits like an angel, trying to draw a picture of a house, tree, and people in the house. It takes forever. Sometimes he looks out the window, sometimes he twiddles the crayons in his hands, and sometimes he squirms in his chair. When the doctor asks to see what he has drawn, Jason is startled, as if suddenly awakened. His drawing is incomplete.

Are Shawn, Melissa, and Jason normal or abnormal? Healthy or sick?

Making an ADD/ADHD diagnosis

It is difficult to draw a clear-cut line between normal and abnormal child behavior. All children are different and behave along a spectrum that ranges from normal to abnormal. Some children are noisy, some calm; some brash and others polite; some are dynamic, while some are passive; still others are gregarious, some shy. Shawn could be a smart, curious child who wants to touch and feel everything around him. Melissa could be a socially immature girl who will mature with time. Jason's classroom inattention may result from his all-absorbing concern about his parents' impending divorce.

But the behaviors of all three children are excessive, pervasive, and persistent. Each one displays these behaviors everywhere: at home, in school, in restaurants, in the grocery store, at relatives' homes. They are failing in school and having problems with their teachers and peers. Their symptoms are not in response to a temporary stressor; they have always been like that. Their parents are exhausted and asking for help. These children have crossed the threshold of normalcy.

Could Shawn, Melissa, and Jason just be acting willfully? Children are programmed to please others. They do not act badly intentionally unless they are "driven" to do so by an underlying disease or condition. Children, innately, want to please others; they yearn for approval and accolades. Shawn,

Melissa, and Jason are not acting willfully. They behave abnormally because they have an underlying behavioral disorder.

> *Attention deficit, or failure to attend to the task at hand, is the cardinal feature of ADD/ADHD.*

Diagnosis of behavioral disorders does not depend upon telltale signs that can be seen, touched, or heard with the stethoscope. It is inferential—an educated guess at best—based upon a constellation of observed behaviors. Isolated behaviors are not diagnostic; but when a set of behaviors occurs together at a degree and frequency such that the child cannot do what is expected of him (e.g., learn in school) or is not able to relate properly to people around him (parents, teachers, or peers), a behavior disorder is diagnosed.

Major symptoms of ADD/ADHD

The children described above are not able to focus and maintain attention, and are easily distracted. All three are impulsive and two are hyperactive. While individually their symptoms are not diagnostic of any disease, together they constitute a disorder called attention deficit disorder (ADD) (also called attention deficit–hyperactive disorder or ADHD). Major symptoms are:

Attention deficit: Attention deficit, or failure to attend to the task at hand, is the cardinal feature of ADD/ADHD. The process of paying attention to a task involves getting tuned into a task and remaining focused on it until the goal is achieved. It is like driving a car: you turn on the ignition (get focused), put the car (body and mind) in proper gear (necessary level of arousal for the task), hold the steering wheel in constant check (stay focused), look at the road ahead (stay vigilant), drive at the right speed (tempo), and reach the destination (complete the task) without getting lost due to distractions (off-task activities).

How much attention a child pays to a task depends upon the nature of the task. If it is pleasing, she will pay attention to it effortlessly. Most children are able to focus on a video game or a television show because they get instant pleasure from them, inviting more viewing (a process called reinforcement).

Moreover, these programs flood their senses with so much input—flooding the gates, as it were—that other distractions cannot enter their brains. The litmus test of ADD/ADHD is the inability to focus on homework or on a task that does not reward the children immediately.

I have seen two types of inattentive children: those who cannot get focused on any task, the "failure-of-ignition" type, and those who cannot stay focused, the "failure-to-drive" type. "Failure-of-ignition" type children either wander aimlessly doing nothing meaningful or sit passively, looking out the window or twiddling their thumbs. They require constant reminders to begin a task, but may finish what they start. Failure-to-drive type children leap like frogs from task to task, failing to finish anything they start. Despite constant reminders, nothing is accomplished. Children who fail to sustain attention are easily bored and need a constant pep talk to keep up their rapidly fading interest. They burn out quickly. The speed and quality of their performance are very inconsistent: sometimes fast, sometimes slow; sometimes good, sometimes poor. They lack the motivation to accomplish something in the distant future.

Attention in a child matures from the exploratory, rapid, impulsive, and reinforcement-based manner of a 2-year-old (requiring constant approval from the parents) to the slow, deliberate, goal-directed, logical, and productive style of a 12-year-old. The attention skills of children with ADD/ADHD do not mature according to this schedule. Their attention remains divergent and, instead of being driven internally by a goal, is driven by constant reinforcement from the environment (context- and contingency-based).

> *// Children with ADD/ADHD have a short circuit in their nerve-cell wiring, causing them to act impulsively. //*

Distractibility: Children with ADD/ADHD have a tendency to get easily distracted by every little noise or movement in their surroundings. To sustain attention to a task, one has to literally shut the gates of the brain so that irrelevant stimuli do not gate crash into conscious awareness. Children with ADD/ADHD are distracted by every sensation that reaches their five senses. Their situation is similar to a radio that has "constant static" even when it is tuned to a particular station. A truck drives by on the road, and children with ADD/ADHD run to the window, leaving their homework. Someone knocks at the door, and they are the first to ask, "Who's there?" When there are no external distractions, they can have a state of internal distractibility, daydreaming and wandering all over the globe.

> **//** *Most children with ADD/ADHD have problems understanding social context and mood.* **//**

The underlying neurological basis of distractibility in children with ADD/ADHD seems to be a lack of sensory filtration at the level of the caudate nucleus, a group of nerve cells in the brain that acts as a relay station for all sensory input before it reaches conscious awareness. Normally, the caudate nucleus serves as a gatekeeper, allowing only relevant stimuli to reach conscious awareness. In children with ADD/ADHD, the head of the right caudate nucleus is small compared with that in normal children and fails to inhibit the onslaught of input from various sense organs on the brain. Every stimulus makes it to conscious awareness.

Impulsivity: Children with ADD/ADHD have a short circuit in their nerve-cell wiring, causing them to act impulsively. They literally respond from the gut, not the mind, and frequently incorrectly. A child with ADD/ADHD is often the first to raise his hand to give an answer to a question, even if he does not know the correct one. He may actually blurt out the answer without even raising his hand. An adolescent with ADD/ADHD may destroy an appliance because she turns it on without reading the instructions. Adults with ADD/ADHD may impulsively buy stock without knowing the fundamentals of the company, simply because they heard someone in the elevator say it is a good buy. Individuals with ADD/ADHD often get into trouble with the law because they act without thinking about the consequences of their actions.

This tendency to act impulsively rather than reflectively is due to poor working memory, resulting in poor processing of incoming information. The working memory cannot simultaneously hold information about prior experience with an action and its likely consequence. In other words, they have no forethought or afterthought.

A related deficit that results in impulsivity is the inability of children with ADD/ADHD to delay gratification and wait their turn. A child with ADD/ADHD who goes to a restaurant with his parents cannot wait patiently to be served. He calls to the waitress many times despite his parents' admonition, twiddles with the silverware until it falls to the floor, and, finally, gets up and pulls at the waitress's dress and demands his food. This is not a "bad" child. Researchers have shown that impulsivity is not a flaw of character, but a defect of biology.

Hyperactivity: Although generally considered to be the most salient feature of this disorder because of its obtrusiveness, this symptom is not present in all ADD/ADHD cases. Hyperactivity can be present in various ways: a macro form, in which children are agitated, restless, and move constantly from place to place, touching people and things; a micro form, in which children squirm and fidget in their seats; and a hyperactive tongue (or hyper-tongue) type, in which children are garrulous, talking excessively, often out of context and interrupting others.

Deficits in the brain's executive functions: Executive functions of the brain involve organization, self-monitoring, self-regulation, and continuous quality-improvement functions similar to those that a manager performs in an office. As children grow and develop, they learn to perform these functions. Children with ADD/ADHD do not.

> **❝** *ADD/ADHD is an equal-opportunity disorder. It is found in all social and economic classes.* **❞**

Because of such deficits, children with ADD/ADHD are not able to organize their space and time well. Their desks and rooms are disorganized. They also cannot self-monitor and self-regulate their actions, whether physical or verbal. They thunder around with no concept of the energy spent or the resulting din, even when admonished that they are making the house shake. In a similar way, their volume control can be on permanent "high."

Another result of such executive function deficits is that children with ADD/ADHD are unable to learn from experience.

Not only are they unable to monitor themselves, they do not respond to admonitions and advice from those in charge. It is difficult for them to follow rules. This makes them hard to discipline and results in conflicts with those in authority. Parents often complain that their child does not listen, is disobedient, and deliberately tries to hurt their feelings. Sadly, once children organize their self-image around these negative behaviors, they deteriorate into opposition, non-compliance, and defiance.

Children with poor executive functions are also clumsy and accident-prone. They neither plan their movements properly nor execute them smoothly. Unable to track their movements within the environment in which they move, they trip over bumps and fall into holes.

Finally, children with deficits in the brain's executive function process incoming information very superficially. It is with great difficulty that things "sink" into their heads. They often misinterpret what others say, which results in conflicts. They are also unable to process the visual information that they get from others' body language—whether others are welcoming their interruption or are getting annoyed. Not only do they not process external information well, they are also unable to interpret the feedback their brains receive from their own ears, eyes, and body. A child who is shouting at the top of her voice, for example, may not be able to appreciate her mom's reprimand that she was screaming.

Social behavior

Deficits of social behavior: Most children with ADD/ADHD have problems understanding social context and mood (poor social cognition) and are unable to match their behavior to them (poor social adaptability). In other words, they are socially inept: they do not understand whether the social mood is grim or jovial, they speak and act without understanding the social situation, they lack social grace, they are awkward and tactless, and they are intrusive and inopportune. These behaviors cause conflicts with their siblings and peers, make them unpopular, and lead to social rejection.

Deficits in this category go beyond mastering social graces, however. Children with ADD/ADHD also have difficulty following instructions. Rules are a mystery to them because:

• they are so inattentive that they do not receive information properly;

- they have difficulty processing the information they receive as instruction; or
- their impulses make it difficult for them to follow the instructions.

Rules are a set of instructions that a child is supposed to follow at home and in school. A particular house may have a rule that toys must be put away in the toy chest before bedtime. Ordinarily, after a few repetitions, this instruction would become part of a child's behavioral dictionary. Children with ADD/ADHD, however, will not be able to internalize it. They may have to be told what is expected of them again and again. This may be a nuisance and an aggravation for parents, who often perceive it as opposition and defiance.

Another deficit in social behavior for children with ADD/ADHD is the lack of both hindsight and foresight: With smaller working memories, they can neither retrieve past experience nor think about future consequences. This accounts for their failure to learn from past mistakes or to plan for the future. They live in the immediate present—moment to moment—driven by their impulses and immediate responses to external stimuli.

Aggression is yet another consequence. Children with ADD/ADHD can indulge in random acts of aggression because of impulsivity and the inability to think of the consequences of their actions. Children who indulge in aggressive acts in a deliberate and premediated manner are likely to have conduct disorder and should be seen by a psychiatrist.

Deficits in social behavior often also cause children with ADD/ADHD to act out in order to be the center of attention. For example, Johnny is the class clown. He laughs, makes faces, grunts, and makes silly comments to get attention. If no one pays attention, he becomes louder and more obtrusive. When he is ignored, he becomes increasingly disruptive, blows on other's faces, touches them, and so on, until they pay attention.

These children also blame others for their own mistakes, are sensitive to criticism, do not accept responsibility for their actions, pout and sulk, and seek attention maladaptively, as a toddler would. For example, a child with ADD/ADHD would blame his peers for his aggressive acts: "I hit him because he was bothering me"; "I yelled at the teacher because he was mean to me." Not only are their actions driven by external contexts and contingencies—phenomena called external locus of control—their sense of responsibility is projected to others as well. They rarely accept moral responsibility for their actions. . . .

An equal-opportunity disorder

ADD/ADHD is an equal-opportunity disorder. It is found in all social and economic classes, from the inner city to the suburbs to the rural countryside. It is equally unconcerned with race or ethnic origin. Nor is ADD/ADHD limited to the United States— it has also been reported in the United Kingdom, Canada, Australia, Spain, and Germany. While reported less often in Europe and Australia than in the US, this may be due to physicians adhering to a more conservative approach to diagnosis and treatment of ADD/ADHD in those countries, as researchers working in the United Kingdom, New Zealand, Australia, and Germany, as well as in the US, have concluded. Because physicians in the US know when and how to look for it, they find it more often than their colleagues in other countries. A closer scrutiny of children's behavior in urban centers of developing countries such as China, Hong Kong, India, and Brazil, for example, has meant a steep rise in the number of children identified with ADD/ADHD. . . .

What can be done about ADD/ADHD

ADD/ADHD is not a death knell for a child's academic, social, or employment future. It is, however, a wake-up call. Once ADD/ADHD has been diagnosed, the strengths and weaknesses of the child should be identified for the purpose of treatment. The ADD/ADHD label should have the sole purpose of helping the child, not to disparage him or her. Labeling should not be stigmatizing and, last but not least, certainly should not decrease either parents' or teachers' expectations—only make them realistic.

2

ADHD Is Overdiagnosed

Michelle Meyer

Michelle Meyer is a writer and frequent contributor to Better Homes and Gardens *magazine.*

Numerous psychologists and doctors believe that many children diagnosed with attention deficit/hyperactivity disorder (ADHD) do not in fact have the condition and are being prescribed drugs unnecessarily. While some of these children suffer from conditions other than ADHD, such as depression or dyslexia, others are being misdiagnosed for simply being bored in school or engaging in typical childhood behavior.

When Sarah Collier's kindergarten teacher suggested she was hyperactive and required medication, her mother, Theresa, fumed inwardly. After taking her own quick time-out to cool off, the Rockford, Illinois, stay-at-home mom calmly coached the teacher on how to handle bubbly Sarah.

Once the girl was seated at the front of the class and given clear directions on what was acceptable in class and what wasn't, she was far less distracted and restless. "Within weeks, she was just fine and the teacher didn't complain again," Theresa says.

That is, until the same teacher had Sarah's younger sister, Haylee, two years later. Once again, Theresa had to steer the conversation away from drugs and toward the same measures that had worked for Sarah. "After summer break, children sometimes need to settle down and get into classroom rhythm," she says. "And teachers need to get used to the new students' temperaments. Kids also have certain ways they learn best."

Neither Sarah, now 8, nor Haylee, 6, went on Attention Deficit/Hyperactivity Disorder (ADHD) drugs and that has them bucking a national trend. Treatment with Ritalin—the most popular drug used to treat ADHD—and its chemical cousins have skyrocketed. Production of these drugs has increased more than fourfold in the last decade, from 11,000 pounds in 1993 to 46,000 pounds in 2002, according to the U.S. Drug Enforcement Administration.

"Children with the slightest attention problem are sent to be assessed for ADHD at our clinic," says William Frankenberger, a psychologist and director of the Human Development Center at the University of Wisconsin–Eau Claire. "We can't believe they were referred. We know the condition is overdiagnosed."

Most referrals to centers like Frankenberger's come at the behest of teachers who have to deal with the disruptions the kids are causing. Estimates show that every classroom in the country has at least one ADHD child, the label for kids who are chronically impulsive, fidgety, or unable to focus. It's the second most common disorder in children, behind only asthma. About 3.8 million kids have ADHD, according to the American Academy of Pediatrics. That number doesn't include the millions more who have occasional symptoms that mimic ADHD, like hyperactivity, but, in fact, are merely kids being kids.

Drugs help some

Despite increasingly widespread concern over ADHD medications being given to some children unnecessarily, drugs have unquestionably helped children who truly do have ADHD. Until Ritalin—the first and still most popular ADHD drug—came on the market in 1957, children unable to concentrate were dubbed daydreamers or troublemakers. They often dropped out of school or drifted to the back of the classroom and the bottom of the bell curve.

> *Treatment with Ritalin—the most popular drug used to treat ADHD—and its chemical cousins have skyrocketed.*

That might have been the fate of Chris, a Chicago-area 6-year-old who was too frenetic to sit still at a desk or write clearly. "I compared his energy to an electric buzz, because you could feel it emanate from him as he ran into walls and crashed off furniture," says Lorna, his stay-at-home mother, who asked that her family's full name not be used.

She tried several nonpharmaceutical remedies with no success. Only after doctors put him on Ritalin did his hyperactivity fade. "The drug made a big difference in his ability to sit still and focus, and even his handwriting improved. He quickly learned to read and soon went from failing to earning A's."

> *What concerns a growing number of experts is that too many kids are on drugs who shouldn't be.*

There's no question some kids need the pills, but what concerns a growing number of experts is that too many kids are on drugs who shouldn't be—either because they have very mild cases of ADHD or, even worse, they don't have ADHD at all.

"In the past, diagnosing ADHD was looked upon with great skepticism, but now it's almost as if any child behavior problem is considered ADHD unless proven otherwise," says Dr. Anthony Rostain, psychiatry education director at the University of Pennsylvania in Philadelphia. "The pendulum has swung too far the other way."

Some blame that pendulum swing on overcrowded classrooms and overworked teachers, where one unruly kid among 30 students can mean chaos. Indeed, a Wisconsin survey of 250 psychologists showed that 77 percent of initial referrals for an ADHD examination came from teachers, not parents.

Others fault busy or overly lax parents who fail to punish misbehavior or teach time-management skills, two parenting flaws that can leave children with behavioral issues that mimic ADHD.

And some argue that doctors cut corners, too, prescribing ADHD drugs solely because a teacher has suggested it (or insisted on it) to a parent, rather than looking into a child's medical, psychological, and developmental history at home as well as at school. Ideally, a pediatrician, psychologist, and learning specialist all should evaluate a child.

If your child's school is pressing for medication, request in writing that the school order a battery of tests to evaluate the child for learning disabilities, a free service to public-school students. You can also consult (at your own expense) a psychologist, who can offer guidance to parents and schools.

Fixing the problem

But whether the rise in use of ADHD medications stems from parents, teachers, or doctors—or a combination of all three—fixing the problem requires time and energy. Writing a prescription does not.

"Addressing those problems is labor-intensive and can take months of constant attention," says Dr. Marianne Zura, a pediatrician at the Medical College of Georgia Children's Medical Center in Augusta. Drugs, by contrast, have immediate results.

ADHD is also commonly misdiagnosed, says Rostain. Depression, anxiety, bipolar disorder, dyslexia, and even poor vision or hearing can be wrongly diagnosed as ADHD. Many of these disorders share symptoms, such as inattentiveness, insomnia, impulsiveness, and unruliness. The label also may be misapplied to kids who are bright and bored, or those struggling with memorization skills or a family crisis, such as divorce.

In the latest rush to prescribe drugs, it's also sometimes forgotten that almost all preschoolers are extremely active with short attention spans, thus the U.S. Food and Drug Administration discourages ADHD drug use under age 6.

Yet Claire Oshetsky of San Jose, California, was ordered to have her 2-year-old son, Paul, treated for ADHD or leave his nursery school. Paul reverted to his usual sweet personality once placed in a preschool with fewer rules and more time outdoors. "I came away convinced that if you put a child in the right environment, he will flourish. Parents should trust their own instincts," says Claire.

That's what Judy McMordie, from Adrian, Michigan, did after sons Tucker and Denver were labeled ADHD. Denver was placed on Ritalin and Tucker on a trio of drugs, none of which helped.

Yet despite the lack of improvement, doctors continued recommending pills, without further testing. Finally, the family's eye doctor diagnosed Tucker, now 12, and Denver, 9, with vision problems.

"Their eyes don't relay to their brain what they're seeing—and that's why they're having difficulties learning," their mother says. "It's an ongoing fight with the schools, who want me to put my children back on the drugs, and I refuse. I care about my children's long-term well-being—not a quick fix for their teachers. I think schools have become drug pushers."

Side effects of drugs

Judy's desire to keep her kids off medication comes in part from concerns over what those medications do. The use of ADHD drugs has been proven safe for the vast majority of kids by decades of use, but that doesn't mean they are without side effects.

In a study of 560 Wisconsin students led by the University of Wisconsin's Frankenberger, 64 percent of the kids on drugs said they experienced side effects sometimes and 30 percent "almost always." More than half complained of insomnia, 54 percent of loss of appetite, and 40 percent of facial tics.

The drugs can also cause stunted growth and seizures in a very small number of cases. Kids often experience dizziness, weight loss, racing heartbeat, and headaches.

Yet doctors sometimes don't check in with kids after prescribing medications. "It's critical for the clinician to ask the child and parent about the side effects," says Dr. Timothy Wilens, a Harvard University child psychiatrist and author of *Straight Talk About Psychiatric Medications for Kids*. "The medicines should bring out the true child; they should not be chemical straitjackets."

Even if your child is one of the many who should be on medication, it need not be a lifelong sentence, says Dr. Sarabjit Singh, medical director of the Disruptive Behavior Disorder Clinic at Children's Hospital of New York–Presbyterian at Columbia University.

Though ADHD is a chronic disorder, once kids reach 12 or 13, they may outgrow the need for drugs. "What happens is, you learn to adapt to the condition, to cope with symptoms," he says.

Whatever you decide to do, make sure that your instincts as a parent are heeded just as well as the suggestions of a doctor or teacher. That gut feeling might just pay off, as Theresa Collier can attest.

To this day, Haylee and Sarah are doing just fine without drugs. "They aren't behind in class," Theresa says. "If they really were ADHD, I think they'd have had more learning or behavior problems."

3

ADHD Is a Hoax

Fred A. Baughman Jr., interviewed by Kelly Patricia O'Meara

Fred A. Baughman Jr. is a retired neurologist. Kelly Patricia O'Meara is an investigative reporter for the magazine Insight on the News.

Attention deficit/hyperactivity disorder (ADHD) is a hoax perpetuated by the psychiatric community and pharmaceutical companies. There is no scientific proof that such a disease exists as a real disorder of the brain. Children who are labeled with the disorder are being victimized.

Retired California neurologist Fred A. Baughman Jr. fired off a letter in January 2000 to U.S. Surgeon General David Satcher in response to Satcher's *Report on Mental Illness*. "Having gone to medical school," Baughman wrote, "and studied pathology—disease, then diagnosis—you and I and all physicians know that the presence of any bona fide disease, like diabetes, cancer or epilepsy, is confirmed by an objective finding—a physical or chemical abnormality. No demonstrable physical or chemical abnormality: no disease!

"You also know, I am sure," Baughman continued, "that there is no physical or chemical abnormality to be found in life, or at autopsy, in 'depression, bipolar disorder and other mental illnesses.' Why then are you telling the American people that 'mental illnesses' are 'physical' and that they are due to 'chemical disorders?'"

Baughman concluded his six-page letter to Satcher by saying that "your role in this deception and victimization is clear. Whether you are a physician so unscientific that you cannot read their [the American Psychiatric Association's] contrived, 'neurobiologic' literature and see the fraud, or whether you see it and choose to be an accomplice—you should resign."

It is this direct, no-nonsense style that has made Baughman a pariah among the psychiatric and mental-health communities and a hero to families of children across America who believe they have been "victimized" by the attention-deficit/hyperactivity disorder (ADHD) label. The "disease," Baughman tells *Insight*, "is a total 100 percent fraud," and he has made it his personal "crusade" to bring an end to the ADHD diagnosis.

Interviewing Dr. Baughman

Insight: You've spent 35 years in private practice as an adult and child neurologist, diagnosing real diseases. What spurred your interest in the ADHD diagnosis?

Fred A. Baughman Jr.: Through the 1970s and 1980s the ADHD "epidemic" began to impact all of us, and the numbers of children being referred to me were increasing dramatically, I'd examine these kids to determine whether they did or did not have real diseases. After giving them thorough examinations, doing such tests as I deemed were necessary, I couldn't find anything wrong with them.

Psychiatry never has proved that ADHD . . . even exists.

I was becoming more and more aware that something was afoot from the tone with which the diagnoses were being made in schools and by psychiatrists who were part of the school team. And never mind that I could find no scientific basis for the diagnosis. But here were pediatricians and school psychiatrists practicing mental health in ways that did not make sense. Principals and teachers would threaten that if I didn't diagnose ADHD they'd find someone who would. As a neurologist, I'm in the business of diagnosing real diseases, so this attitude on the part of people who should know better was very disturbing.

You are among a small number of physicians publicly to challenge the psychiatric community about this diagnosis. Why do you think so many doctors are diagnosing ADHD when they, too, must know there is no scientific data to support it?

Most physicians, like the public, have bought into the whole psychiatric line. The populace at large has been so brainwashed by this "tyranny of the experts" that they cannot bring themselves to believe things are other than what the psychiatric industry and the pharmaceutical companies tell them. The population has been told again and again that these "diseases" exist, despite the fact that there is no scientific proof to back up their claims.

Lies of psychiatry

People have been lied to so often that they can't disabuse themselves of the notion that these so-called diseases are chemical abnormalities of the brain. Psychiatry never has proved that ADHD, let alone depression, anxiety or obsessive-compulsive disorder [OCD], even exists. Yet this hasn't stopped doctors from diagnosing them. It simply was decided during the early days of psychopharmacology—of psychiatric drugs—that these were nice theories and they were fed to the public as fact.

With the diagnosis comes the "fix," the prescription pills that reportedly help control these diseases.

Yes, that's right, and like the unscientific diagnosis no one really knows how these drugs work on the brain. It's all just theory at this point.

But then this same psychiatric community says even depression is a disease resulting from a chemical imbalance. They also say that OCD is a disease with a known chemical abnormality of the brain. In neither case is there proof to support either claim. Through the years, though, they've gotten to fudging their line a bit, saying instead: "Well, it's a psychiatric disorder."

You've testified before Congress on this issue, and several of your papers on these matters have been published in medical journals. Recently you traveled to France to address a committee of the Parliamentary Assembly of the Council of France as a counterweight to ADHD advocates. What kind of response did you get?

I was charged with presenting the argument against the diagnosis and treatment of ADHD. I never expected it to go so well.

Three European psychiatrists presented the case for the ADHD diagnosis using the same old slide-show presentation, presumably showing brain atrophy in the patients diagnosed with ADHD.

I pointed out to them, as I've done numerous times here in the states, that all the patients in the slides whose brains showed atrophy also had been on stimulant therapy, so there was no way to know that the atrophy was not, in fact, caused by the drugs rather than the alleged brain disorder ADHD. A member of the council committee summarized what had transpired during the day and basically said they didn't believe what the psychiatrists had presented about ADHD—that they were skeptical about the appropriateness of the drugs recommended for the diagnosis.

> *People are being told in no uncertain terms that this 'disease' exists and should be treated with drugs, so it's extremely difficult to get the truth out.*

One of the psychiatrists was so intimidated by my argument that he threatened to leave the meeting. It was just amazing to see this guy get so frazzled. The council was terrific, and I couldn't have imagined so favorable a response. It was so unlike a typical U.S. response. I think the Europeans are trying to resist this whole ADHD business.

You set up a Website, www.adhdfraud.org, to help get information out to parents who have been impacted by the ADHD diagnosis. What kind of response are you getting from parents?

Families being victimized

I hear from many families who have been victimized by this diagnosis. By the time they find me their eyes usually have been opened and they realize the fraud of the diagnosis. But they also realize how serious the diagnosis is for the child and the problems it can create for families.

On the other side of the coin, of course, are the perpetrators at the National Institute of Mental Health [NIMH] and the academic psychiatrists who put out the ADHD propaganda. These people also know who I am and try not to respond to the letters and papers I write. They don't want to see me at medical conferences and seminars because they know that I have the facts, take no prisoners and am willing to show that they are perpetrating a fraud. If they can keep the public in the dark about the facts of this alleged "disease" then science is beside the point.

I'd love to debate the surgeon general or anyone in the hierarchy of academic psychiatry, but I don't think any would agree. The surgeon general wouldn't even respond to the letter I wrote to him about his *Report on Mental Illness*, so I don't see him stepping up to the plate anytime soon.

You've testified in court for nearly two dozen families who were fighting the ADHD diagnosis. What should parents do when their child has been diagnosed?

People are being told in no uncertain terms that this "disease" exists and should be treated with drugs, so it's extremely difficult to get the truth out. The essential first step of the perpetrators is to label the child with ADHD. I've seen how these things turn out for those who try to go up against the system, and it is very sad. Before parents find themselves in a legal adversarial relationship with the school system and county officials, they should get their child out of that school and either homeschool them or put them into a parochial or private school. I tell parents with children caught up in this fraud that, for now, going against the system is a no-win situation.

What will it take to turn the establishment crowd on this issue?

I'm trying to expose the medical fraud and to get just and appropriate medical treatment for children when it is needed and, where it isn't required, I'm trying to get appropriate education, parenting, disciplining and training so these children can achieve self-control. They all certainly are capable of it.

We've got to do something because we're talking about 6 million to 8 million children who have been diagnosed with ADHD. This just can't wait.

4

ADHD Is Not a Myth or Hoax

Michael Fumento

Michael Fumento is a journalist and science writer whose books include Science Under Seige *and* Bioevolution: How Biotechnology Is Changing Our World.

Many conservative writers and commentators have argued that attention deficit/hyperactivity disorder (ADHD) may be a hoax and call it a prime example of the unwelcome societal trend of turning discipline problems into pathological medical disorders. Some of these same critics have compared ADHD medications with illegal drugs such as cocaine and argue that their use should be discouraged. However, there is ample scientific and medical evidence that ADHD is a real disorder and that Ritalin and similar drugs really do work in helping children and their families. Those with personal or family experience with ADHD can especially attest that it is not a myth.

It's both right-wing and vast, but it's not a conspiracy. Actually, it's more of an anti-conspiracy. The subject is Attention Deficit Disorder (ADD) and Attention Deficit Hyperactivity Disorder (ADHD), closely related ailments (henceforth referred to in this article simply as ADHD). Rush Limbaugh declares it "may all be a hoax." Francis Fukuyama devotes much of one chapter in his latest book, *Our Posthuman Future* to attacking Ritalin, the top-selling drug used to treat ADHD. Columnist Thomas Sowell writes, "The motto used to be: 'Boys will be boys.' Today, the motto seems to be: 'Boys will be medicated.'" And

Phyllis Schlafly explains, "The old excuse of 'my dog ate my homework' has been replaced by 'I got an ADHD diagnosis.'" A March 2002 article in *The Weekly Standard* summed up the conservative line on ADHD with this rhetorical question: "Are we really prepared to redefine childhood as an ailment, and medicate it until it goes away?"

Many conservative writers, myself included, have criticized the growing tendency to pathologize every undesirable behavior—especially where children are concerned. But, when it comes to ADHD, this skepticism is misplaced. As even a cursory examination of the existing literature or, for that matter, simply talking to the parents and teachers of children with ADHD reveals, the condition is real, and it is treatable. And, if you don't believe me, you can ask conservatives who've come face to face with it themselves.

A real disorder

Myth: ADHD isn't a real disorder.

The most common argument against ADHD on the right is also the simplest: It doesn't exist. Conservative columnist Jonah Goldberg thus reduces ADHD to "ants in the pants." Sowell equates it with "being bored and restless." Fukuyama protests, "No one has been able to identify a cause of ADD/ADHD. It is a pathology recognized only by its symptoms." And a conservative columnist approvingly quotes Thomas Armstrong, Ritalin opponent and author, when he declares, "ADD is a disorder that cannot be authoritatively identified in the same way as polio, heart disease or other legitimate illnesses."

> *A cursory examination of the existing literature . . . reveals, the condition is real, and it is treatable.*

The Armstrong and Fukuyama observations are as correct as they are worthless. "Half of all medical disorders are diagnosed without benefit of a lab procedure," notes Dr. Russell Barkley, professor of psychology at the College of Health Professionals at the Medical University of South Carolina. "Where are the lab tests for headaches and multiple sclerosis and Alzheimer's?" he asks. "Such a standard would virtually eliminate all mental disorders."

Often the best diagnostic test for an ailment is how it responds to treatment. And, by that standard, it doesn't get much more real than ADHD. The beneficial effects of administering stimulants to treat the disorder were first reported in 1937. And today medication for the disorder is reported to be 75 to 90 percent successful. "In our trials it was close to ninety percent," says Dr. Judith Rapoport, director of the National Institute of Mental Health's Child Psychiatry Branch, who has published about 100 papers on ADHD. "This means there was a significant difference in the children's ability to function in the classroom or at home."

Additionally, epidemiological evidence indicates that ADHD has a powerful genetic component. University of Colorado researchers have found that a child whose identical twin has the disorder is between eleven and 18 times more likely to also have it than is a non-twin sibling. For these reasons, the American Psychiatric Association (APA), American Medical Association, American Academy of Pediatrics, American Academy of Child Adolescent Psychiatry, the surgeon general's office, and other major medical bodies all acknowledge ADHD as both real and treatable.

> *Epidemiological evidence indicates that ADHD has a powerful genetic component.*

Myth: ADHD is part of a feminist conspiracy to make little boys more like little girls.

Many conservatives observe that boys receive ADHD diagnoses in much higher numbers than girls and find in this evidence of a feminist conspiracy. (This, despite the fact that genetic diseases are often heavily weighted more toward one gender or the other.) Sowell refers to "a growing tendency to treat boyhood as a pathological condition that requires a new three R's—repression, re-education and Ritalin." Fukuyama claims Prozac is being used to give women "more of the alpha-male feeling," while Ritalin is making boys act more like girls. "Together, the two sexes are gently nudged toward that androgynous median personality . . . that is the current politically cor-

rect outcome in American society." George Will, while ac-
knowledging that Ritalin can be helpful, nonetheless writes of
the "androgyny agenda" of "drugging children because they are
behaving like children, especially boy children." Anti-Ritalin
conservatives frequently invoke Christina Hoff Sommers's best-
selling 2000 book, *The War Against Boys*. You'd never know that
the drug isn't mentioned in her book—or why.

"Originally I was going to have a chapter on it," Sommers
tells me. "It seemed to fit the thesis." What stopped her was
both her survey of the medical literature and her own empiri-
cal findings. Of one child she personally came to know she
says, "He was utterly miserable, as was everybody around him.
The drugs saved his life."

Blaming schools and parents

*Myth: ADHD is part of the public school system's efforts to ware-
house kids rather than to discipline and teach them.*

"No doubt life is easier for teachers when everyone sits
around quietly," writes Sowell. Use of ADHD drugs is "in the
school's interest to deal with behavioral and discipline problems [because] it's so easy to use Ritalin to make kids compliant: to get them to sit down, shut up, and do what they're
told," declares Schlafly. The word "zombies" to describe children under the effects of Ritalin is tossed around more than in
a B-grade voodoo movie.

Kerri Houston, national field director for the American
Conservative Union and the mother of two ADHD children on
medication, agrees with much of the criticism of public
schools. "But don't blame ADHD on crummy curricula and
lazy teachers," she says. "If you've worked with these children,
you know they have a serious neurological problem." In any
case, Ritalin, when taken as prescribed, hardly stupefies children. To the extent the medicine works, it simply turns ADHD
children into normal children. "ADHD is like having thirty
televisions on at one time, and the medicine turns off twenty-
nine so you can concentrate on the one," Houston describes.
"This zombie stuff drives me nuts! My kids are both as lively
and as fun as can be."

*Myth: Parents who give their kids anti-ADHD drugs are merely
doping up problem children.*

Limbaugh calls ADHD "the perfect way to explain the inattention, incompetence, and inability of adults to control their

kids." Addressing parents directly, he lectures, "It helped you mask your own failings by doping up your children to calm them down."

Such charges blast the parents of ADHD kids into high orbit. That includes my Hudson Institute colleague (and fellow conservative) Mona Charen, the mother of an eleven-year-old with the disorder. "I have two non-ADHD children, so it's not a matter of parenting technique," says Charen. "People without such children have no idea what it's like. I can tell the difference between boyish high spirits and pathological hyperactivity. . . . These kids bounce off the walls. Their lives are chaos; their rooms are chaos. And nothing replaces the drugs."

Barkley and Rapoport say research backs her up. Randomized, controlled studies in both the United States and Sweden have tried combining medication with behavioral interventions and then dropped either one or the other. For those trying to go on without medicine, "the behavioral interventions maintained nothing," Barkley says. Rapoport concurs: "Unfortunately, behavior modification doesn't seem to help with ADHD." (Both doctors are quick to add that ADHD is often accompanied by other disorders that are treatable through behavior modification in tandem with medicine.)

Defending Ritalin

Myth: Ritalin is "kiddie cocaine."

One of the paradoxes of conservative attacks on Ritalin is that the drug is alternately accused of turning children into brain-dead zombies and of making them Mach-speed cocaine junkies. Indeed, Ritalin is widely disparaged as "kiddie cocaine." Writers who have sought to lump the two drugs together include Schlafly, talk-show host and columnist Armstrong Williams, and others whom I hesitate to name because of my long-standing personal relationships with them.

Mary Eberstadt wrote the "authoritative" Ritalin-cocaine piece for the April 1999 issue of *Policy Review*, then owned by the Heritage Foundation. The article, "Why Ritalin Rules," employs the word "cocaine" no fewer than twelve times. Eberstadt quotes from a 1995 Drug Enforcement Agency (DEA) background paper declaring methylphenidate, the active ingredient in Ritalin, "a central nervous system (CNS) stimulant [that] shares many of the pharmacological effects of amphetamine, methamphetamine, and cocaine." Further, it "produces behavioral, psychological, subjective, and reinforcing effects similar to those of d-amphetamine including increases in rating of euphoria, drug liking and activity, and decreases in sedation." Add to this the fact that the Controlled Substances Act lists it as a Schedule II drug, imposing on it the same tight prescription controls as morphine, and Ritalin starts to sound spooky indeed.

> *Where conservatives go wrong is in making ADHD a scapegoat for frustration over what we perceive as a breakdown in the order of society and family.*

What Eberstadt fails to tell readers is that the DEA description concerns methylphenidate abuse. It's tautological to say abuse is harmful. According to the DEA, the drugs in question are comparable when "administered the same way at comparable doses." But ADHD stimulants, when taken as prescribed, are neither administered in the same way as cocaine nor at comparable doses. "What really counts," says Barkley, "is the speed with which the drugs enter and clear the brain. With cocaine, because it's snorted, this happens tremendously quickly, giving users the characteristic addictive high." (Ever seen anyone pop a cocaine tablet?) Further, he says, "There's no evidence anywhere in literature of [Ritalin's] addictiveness when taken as prescribed." As to the Schedule II listing, again this is because of the potential for it to fall into the hands of abusers, not because of its effects on persons for whom it is prescribed. Ritalin and the other anti-ADHD drugs, says Barkley, "are the safest drugs in all of psychiatry." (And they may be getting even safer: A new medicine just released [in February 2003] called Strattera represents the first true non-stimulant ADHD treatment.)

Indeed, a study just released in the journal *Pediatrics*, found that children who take Ritalin or other stimulants to control ADHD cut their risk of future substance abuse by 50 percent compared with untreated ADHD children. The lead author speculated that "by treating ADHD you're reducing the demoralization that accompanies this disorder, and you're improving the academic functioning and well-being of adolescents and young adults during the critical times when substance abuse starts."

Myth: Ritalin is overprescribed across the country.

Some call it "the Ritalin craze." In *The Weekly Standard*, Melana Zyla Vickers informs us that "Ritalin use has exploded," while Eberstadt writes that "Ritalin use more than doubled in the first half of the decade alone, [and] the number of school-children taking the drug may now, by some estimates, be approaching the 4 million mark."

A report in the January 2003 issue of *Archives of Pediatrics and Adolescent Medicine* did find a large increase in the use of ADHD medicines from 1987 to 1996, an increase that doesn't appear to be slowing. Yet nobody thinks it's a problem that routine screening for high blood pressure has produced a big increase in the use of hypertension medicine. "Today, children suffering from ADHD are simply less likely to slip through the cracks," says Dr. Sally Satel, a psychiatrist . . . and author of *PC, M.D.: How Political Correctness Is Corrupting Medicine.*

Satel agrees that some community studies, by the standards laid down in the APA's Diagnostic and Statistical Manual of Mental Disorders (DSM), indicate that ADHD may often be over-diagnosed. On the other hand, she says, additional evidence shows that in some communities ADHD is *under*-diagnosed and *under*-treated. "I'm quite concerned with children who need the medication and aren't getting it," she says.

There are tremendous disparities in the percentage of children taking ADHD drugs when comparing small geographical areas. Psychologist Gretchen LeFever, for example, has compared the number of prescriptions in mostly white Virginia Beach, Virginia, with other, more heavily African American areas in the southeastern part of the state. Conservatives have latched onto her higher numbers—20 percent of white fifth-grade boys in Virginia Beach are being treated for ADHD—as evidence that something is horribly wrong. But others, such as Barkley, worry about the lower numbers. According to LeFever's study, black children are only half as likely to get medication as white children. "Black people don't get the care of white people; children of well-off parents get far better care than those of poorer parents," says Barkley.

Reforming state laws

Myth: States should pass laws that restrict schools from recommending Ritalin.

Conservative writers have expressed delight that several

states, led by Connecticut, have passed or are considering laws ostensibly protecting students from schools that allegedly pass out Ritalin like candy. Representative Lenny Winkler, lead sponsor of the Connecticut measure, told Reuters Health, "If the diagnosis is made, and it's an appropriate diagnosis that Ritalin be used, that's fine. But I have also heard of many families approached by the school system [who are told] that their child cannot attend school if they're not put on Ritalin."

Two attorneys I interviewed who specialize in child-disability issues, including one from the liberal Bazelon Center for Mental Health Law in Washington, D.C., acknowledge that school personnel have in some cases stepped over the line. But legislation can go too far in the other direction by declaring, as Connecticut's law does, that "any school personnel [shall be prohibited] from recommending the use of psychotropic drugs for any child." The law appears to offer an exemption by declaring, "The provisions of this section shall not prohibit *school medical staff* from recommending that a child be evaluated by an appropriate medical practitioner, or prohibit school personnel from consulting with such practitioner, with the consent of the parent or guardian of such child." [Emphasis added.] But of course many, if not most, schools have perhaps one nurse on regular "staff." That nurse will have limited contact with children in the classroom situations where ADHD is likely to be most evident. And, given the wording of the statute, a teacher who believed a student was suffering from ADHD would arguably be prohibited from referring that student to the nurse. Such ambiguity is sure to have a chilling effect on any form of intervention or recommendation by school personnel.

> *Like most headaches, ADHD is a neurological problem that can usually be successfully treated with a chemical.*

Moreover, 20-year special-education veteran Sandra Rief said in an interview with the National Education Association that "recommending medical intervention for a student's behavior could lead to personal liability issues." Teachers, in other words, could be forced to choose between what they think is best for the health of their students and the possible risk of losing not only their jobs but their personal assets as well.

"Certainly it's not within the purview of a school to say kids can't attend if they don't take drugs," says Houston. "On the other hand, certainly teachers should be able to advise parents as to problems and potential solutions. . . . [T]hey may see things parents don't. My own son is an angel at home but was a demon at school."

If the real worry is "take the medicine or take a hike" ultimatums, legislation can be narrowly tailored to prevent them; broad-based gag orders, such as Connecticut's, are a solution that's worse than the problem.

The conservative case for ADHD drugs

There are kernels of truth to every conservative suspicion about ADHD. Who among us has not had lapses of attention? And isn't hyperactivity a normal condition of childhood when compared with deskbound adults? Certainly there are lazy teachers, warehousing schools, androgyny-pushing feminists, and far too many parents unwilling or unable to expend the time and effort to raise their children properly, even by their own standards. Where conservatives go wrong is in making ADHD a scapegoat for frustration over what we perceive as a breakdown in the order of society and family. In a column in *The Boston Herald*, Boston University Chancellor John Silber rails that Ritalin is "a classic example of a cheap fix: low-cost, simple and purely superficial."

Exactly. Like most headaches, ADHD is a neurological problem that can usually be successfully treated with a chemical. Those who recommend or prescribe ADHD medicines do not, as *The Weekly Standard* put it, see them as "discipline in pill-form." They see them as pills.

In fact, it can be argued that the use of those pills, far from being liable for or symptomatic of the Decline of the West, reflects and reinforces conservative values. For one thing, they increase personal responsibility by removing an excuse that children (and their parents) can fall back on to explain misbehavior and poor performance. "Too many psychologists and psychiatrists focus on allowing patients to justify to themselves their troubling behavior," says Satel. "But something like Ritalin actually encourages greater autonomy because you're treating a compulsion to behave in a certain way. Also, by treating ADHD, you remove an opportunity to explain away bad behavior."

Moreover, unlike liberals, who tend to downplay differences between the sexes, conservatives are inclined to believe that there are substantial physiological differences—differences such as boys' greater tendency to suffer ADHD. "Conservatives celebrate the physiological differences between boys and girls and eschew the radical-feminist notion that gender differences are created by societal pressures," says Houston regarding the fuss over the boy-girl disparity among ADHD diagnoses. "ADHD is no exception."

But, however compatible conservatism may be with taking ADHD seriously, the truth is that most conservatives remain skeptics. "I'm sure I would have been one of those smug conservatives saying it's a made-up disease," admits Charen, "if I hadn't found out the hard way." Here's hoping other conservatives find an easier route to accepting the truth.

5

ADHD May Have a Genetic Basis

Brown University Child and Adolescent Behavior Newsletter

The Brown University Child and Adolescent Behavior Newsletter *is produced and edited by professors at the Brown University School of Medicine in Providence, Rhode Island.*

Interviews with three prominent researchers involved in attention deficit/hyperactivity disorder (ADHD) research reveal current scientific thought on the genetics of ADHD. The disorder is highly inheritable and travels along biological family lines. There is evidence linking several specific genes, including the D4 dopamine receptor gene, to the disease, and scientists are searching for other genes involved. Researchers hope that establishing the genetic basis for ADHD will help lessen the stigma attached to the disease.

*R*esearchers are actively investigating the genetic basis for attention-deficit/hyperactivity disorder (ADHD). The accumulation of published reports on the search for genes associated with ADHD, while exciting, can be intimidating and confusing. . . . We asked three researchers involved in ADHD research to sort through the data and summarize briefly where we are in the search for the specific genes linked to ADHD.

We interviewed F. Xavier Castellanos, M.D., Chief, ADHD Research Unit, Child Psychiatry Branch, National Institute of Mental Health; Stephen V. Faraone, Ph.D., Co-editor, Neuropsychiatric Genetics and Associate Professor, Department of Psychiatry, Harvard

Brown University Child and Adolescent Newsletter, "The Search for a Genetic Basis for ADHD Simplified," vol. 17, May 2001. Copyright © 2001 by Manisses Communications Group. Reproduced by permission.

Medical School; and, Cathy L. Barr, Ph.D., Assistant Professor, Department of Psychiatry, The University of Toronto and Scientist at the Toronto Western Hospital in Ontario.

The etiology of ADHD is likely multifactorial, combining genetic, environmental and other risk factors. We asked Castellanos about the difficulty of searching for the cause of this disease.

"It is not yet clear whether there are several etiologically distinct forms of ADHD. However, there is no reason to think that ADHD will be different from other complex conditions, all of which seem to have a range of possible causes, functioning through a number of pathways," said Castellanos.

When asked "What do we know today about the genetics of ADHD," Faraone listed four points:

- "ADHD is highly heritable. About 70 percent of the variance is attributed to genes.
- "Adoption studies show the disorder travels along biological family lines, not adoptive family lines.
- "Persistent ADHD appears to be a highly familial subtype of ADHD.
- "There is strong evidence for an association between ADHD and the D4 dopamine receptor gene (DRD4). The evidence for the dopamine transporter gene (DAT1) is suggestive, but not as strong."

Barr says, "I would say that the molecular genetics studies have made a strong start and that the DRD4 and DAT1 genes look very promising. For any genetic finding, there must be extensive replication before a finding can be accepted. Then, further molecular work must be done to understand the association or linkage finding."

> *The evidence for a genetic basis to ADHD is strong.*

In the January [2001] issue of *The Journal of the American Academy of Child and Adolescent Psychiatry*, Barr noted in a commentary on ADHD and the dopamine D4 receptor gene that, while studies do support DRD4 as a genetic susceptibility factor in ADHD, the findings aren't robust. She wrote: "It is clear that the 7-repeat allele is neither necessary nor sufficient to cause

ADHD and that this is not a straightforward relationship. There-fore, it is still imperative to consider that ADHD is a complex trait and much more evidence needs to be accumulated before we can be conclusive about DRD4 or any gene in this disorder."

Still, everyone we consulted all agreed that the evidence for a genetic basis to ADHD is strong. "It is as strong for ADHD as it is for schizophrenia or bipolar disorder, which is very strong," say Faraone.

Castellanos sums up the feeling, saying, "We're just happy to have some positive replicated results; it's still going to be a long and interesting adventure."

A genetic susceptibility to ADHD does not exclude other causal factors, all three are quick to add. The twin studies sug-gest that the susceptibility factors for ADHD are both genetic and environmental, says Barr. Faraone adds that such factors as social adversity, obstetric complications and exposure to nico-tine as a fetus may be factors related to ADHD. Castellanos lists events that affect brain development in utero or later, such as car accidents and strokes, as documented causes of ADHD.

The DRD4 and DAT1 genes

If there is a strong genetic linkage, there must be specific genes involved. Because most drugs used to treat ADHD affect the dopamine pathway, geneticists have looked for genes involved in this pathway, one of which is the DRD4 and another being the DAT1.

Barr explains that five dopamine receptors (D1–D5) have been cloned, each produced by a different gene. The D2–D4 re-ceptors are thought to be inhibitory. Changes in gene se-quences can arise from mutations. If a variation becomes fre-quent enough that it is encountered in over 1 percent of the population, it is termed a polymorphism. Polymorphisms are important in genetic research, as they serve as markers to help localize genes that may cause or contribute to the expression of an illness. Finding an association between a polymorphism and a disorder suggests that the gene containing the polymor-phism, or a nearby gene, may be involved in causing or con-tributing to the disorder.

Research has shown that DNA changes in the DRD4 and DAT1 genes are associated with a slightly increased risk of man-ifesting ADHD for some individuals. The DAT1 gene allele may be associated with increased reuptake of dopamine and the

DRD4 gene allele may be associated with a subsensitive postsynaptic receptor.

This of course does not exclude other genes in the dopamine pathway and other genes related to different transmitters such as the noradrenergic, serotonergic or cholinergic pathways. These areas have not yet been explored. Castellanos, Faraone and Barr agree that much research lies ahead—and finding specific genes involved takes a lot of time.

> *A genetic susceptibility to ADHD does not exclude other causal factors.*

"Without doubt, these are not the only genes [involved]," says Castellanos. "The question is, how to find the others. One approach is to look throughout the haystack—positional cloning. The other is to continue searching through the usual suspects—candidate genes. Both approaches will likely be important," says Castellanos.

(Positional cloning is finding the position of susceptibility genes based on sharing of chromosomal regions in people with ADHD. This involves searching widely spaced markers throughout the entire genome, and focusing in on suggestive areas with more closely spaced markers. Candidate gene approaches begin by selecting genes likely to be involved based on theories of pathophysiology.)

"The method of action of drugs is a good place to start [looking for specific genes] but, because brain mechanisms are complicated, dopamine is unlikely to tell the full story," says Faraone. He adds that some drugs that have suggested some benefit, such as tricyclics and tomoxetine, have a primarily noradrenergic effect. Cholinergic enhancers, such as nicotine, ABT418 and donepezil, suggest some benefit in treating ADHD as well.

Barr adds, "It is a good bet that the dopamine system is involved, but it may not be the only system. Due to the extensive interaction of the neurotransmitter systems, the genetic changes may be at one site and medications work at another place in the pathway."

For example, Castellanos points out that "diuretics relieve congestive heart failure by promoting urine output, not through direct effects on the heart."

Benefits of finding genes

Although there will be many benefits of discovering specific genes associated with ADHD, developing predictive genetic tests for ADHD is not likely to be one of them.

"I feel the most helpful outcome of determining the genetic basis of ADHD will be that there will be more understanding that this is a biological condition and that it does run in families," she says. "There should not be any stigma associated with having ADHD and parents should feel no different about seeking help for their child than they would for a medical condition."

"Finding a gene and its relevant mutations will provide insights into pathophysiologic pathways which in turn will help the development of new medicines," says Faraone.

Castellanos agrees, and also points out that molecular perspectives on ADHD are already beginning to be used in neuroimaging studies. The integration of these novel approaches will eventually lead to a well-grounded understanding of pathophysiology, which is the essential first step for the development of cost-effective strategies aimed at preventing the morbidity associated with this common condition.

6

Attention Deficit Disorder May Be Caused by Stress and Bad Parenting

Mark Nichols

Mark Nichols was a reporter for the Canadian newsmagazine Maclean's.

According to a Vancouver physician, attention deficit disorder (ADD) is not an inherited genetic condition but has its roots in childhood stresses and flawed parent-child relationships that may stunt the development of children's brains. Rather than resorting to Ritalin and other drugs, parents of affected children should reexamine their parenting and lifestyles.

Vancouver physician Gabor Maté has a striking photograph of himself at the age of four months. The infant, held by his mother, gazes unsmilingly and seemingly with apprehension towards the camera. The year is 1944, the place Budapest, Hungary, and visible on his mother's jacket is a Star of David—"the badge of shame Jews had to wear in countries under Nazi rule," Maté notes in his book *Scattered Minds*,[1] in which the photo appears. Even as the picture was snapped, Adolf Eichmann was preparing a plan for the extermination of Hungary's Jews. And

1. published in the United States in 2000 under the title *Scattered: How Attention Deficit Disorder Originates and What You Can Do About It*

the anxious look on Maté's young face, he suggests, reflected his mother's fears of the Nazi death machine. His maternal grandparents perished in the Holocaust, but Maté's immediate family survived and came to Canada in 1957. Maté believes that the Nazi terror may have left a lasting mark on him by crippling at a critical stage in his life any chance of untroubled mother-infant relations. "These were hardly possible," he writes, "given the terrible circumstances, her numbed state of mind and having to concentrate her energies on basic survival."

A controversial theory

Maté's real subject, however, is not the Nazi era, but attention deficit disorder, the cluster of behavioural and personality problems that affects him and an estimated one million other Canadians. ADD symptoms vary, ranging from hyperactivity, impulsiveness and a short attention span to low self-esteem, workaholic tendencies and poor social skills. Maté's book . . . rejects the widely held belief that ADD is largely an inherited genetic condition and argues instead that the roots of the disorder lie in the pressures of modern life, which can disrupt the "attunement" between child and caregiver needed for normal brain development. By challenging the standard view of ADD, *Scattered Minds* is certain to provoke controversy. "A large number of studies point to a strong genetic component in ADD," says Dr. Lily Hechtman, a child psychiatrist who teaches at Montreal's McGill University. "I don't think the evidence supports the hypothesis that ADD is due to parenting."

> *The roots of the disorder lie in the pressures of modern life.*

Maté's theory will undoubtedly disturb parents of ADD children. But Maté, whose own three children have ADD, insists he is not "blaming parents"—his point is that society's stresses can impair the caregiving skills of the most loving mothers and fathers. Maté presents no original research, but cites current information on the brain and developmental psychology, and draws on his experiences as an ADD sufferer and a doctor who treats the disorder.

While disputing the notion that ADD is genetic in origin, Maté does believe some children have an inherited predisposition for ADD—a heightened sensitivity that makes them susceptible to colic, allergies, asthma, ear infections and other maladies. That hypersensitivity, he contends, extends to the emotional realm. Hypersensitive babies, he argues, are acutely affected by mood and facial expressions that can impede the attunement that ideally exists between mother and infant. Citing recent research into human and animal brain development, Maté concludes that a flawed mother-and-infant relationship can stunt development of the brain's prefrontal cortex, the region responsible for impulse control and emotional regulation. The research shows that it is this disturbance, says Maté, "that accounts for virtually all cases of ADD."

Although he suspects that wartime horrors may have contributed to his own ADD, Maté believes that social forces at work today—divorce, families with two working parents, the breakdown of extended family structures and rising stress levels—constitute the underlying causes of ADD. For people with ADD, the problem begins in infancy and continues in childhood and adolescence. "Among the recurrent themes blighting the childhoods of adults I have seen with severe cases of ADD," writes Maté, "are family strife and divorce, adoption, depression—especially in the mother; violence, especially from the father; alcoholism and sexual abuse." And yet, he notes, none of the parents of ADD children referred to him have "ever before been encouraged to look closely at how their emotions, lives and marriages might affect their children."

Questioning the use of Ritalin

Maté thinks it is high time parents—and physicians—did so, rather than resorting to Ritalin and other psychostimulant drugs that can help many children. Though the annual rate of increase appears to be slowing, Canadian physicians wrote 710,000 prescriptions for Ritalin last year [1998], more than twice the number issued in 1994, according to IMS Health Canada, a firm that tracks drug industry trends. Maté acknowledges that drugs can often help ADD sufferers. But he argues that before seeing their children dosed with chemicals, parents should examine their own relations with their afflicted kids—and that schools, despite cost-cutting pressures, need more teachers and experts trained to deal with ADD.

Citing research that suggests that, far from being immutably fixed in childhood, brain circuits can continue to develop in adulthood and beyond, Maté suggests that under the right conditions people with ADD can learn to manage the disorder—and even, to a large extent, "grow out" of it. Maté may be overoptimistic about that, possibly just plain wrong in his basic contentions. Even so, *Scattered Minds* asks questions that deserve to be considered about a debilitating disorder—and the kind of society in which it flourishes.

7

Television Viewing May Cause ADHD Among Children

Norra MacReady

Norra MacReady is a medical writer and editor whose work has appeared in general interest publications such as Glamour *and* Mademoiselle *as well as medical publications including the* British Medical Journal.

According to one study, children exposed to heavy television viewing were more likely to exhibit attentional and behavioral problems years later—problems that correlate with attention deficit/hyperactivity disorder. The study suggests, but does not prove, that television viewing may play a role in causing ADHD in children. Television presents information in short sound bites and may adversely affect the brain development of very young children, some doctors believe. Parents should not let their children under age two watch television.

Early childhood exposure to television is linked to attentional problems a few years later, Dr. Dimitri A. Christakis and colleagues reported.

The relationship was clinically significant and dose dependent. For every hour spent watching television at 1 or 3 years of age, there was a 10% increase in the probability of attentional problems at age 7 years, according to Dr. Christakis.

This is the first study to test—and confirm—the widely held hypothesis that very early television viewing is associated with the subsequent development of inattention, the investigators said.

The findings suggest that inattention should be added to the list of deleterious consequences of excessive early television viewing, which include obesity and violent behavior.

But the investigators stopped short of relating TV watching to full-blown attention-deficit hyperactivity disorder (ADHD). "We only looked at parental reports of attentional problems, and the specific symptoms that parents were queried about were many of the core symptoms of attention-deficit disorder," Dr. Christakis, director of the Child Health Institute at the University of Washington, Seattle, told this newspaper [*Pediatric News*].

"But this is not a clinical diagnosis, which requires input from parents and teachers. We had no input from teachers at all," he said.

The data

The data came from the National Longitudinal Survey of Youth 1979 (NLSY79) Children and Young Adults, a nationwide survey of more than 11,000 children that began in 1986 and is updated biennially. The current analysis consisted of data on children who were at or near 7 years of age in 1996, 1998, or 2000.

Attentional problem status was derived from the hyperactivity subscale of the Behavior Problems Index, which contains items asking about the child's impulsivity, restlessness, and ability to concentrate. The information was obtained from the children's mothers. In each survey, the mothers were also asked to estimate the amount of time their children watched television each day.

> *Early childhood exposure to television is linked to attentional problems a few years later.*

The main prediction variable was the number of hours the children watched television daily at ages 1 and 3 years.

"We chose these two ages because they precede the age at which attentional problems are typically manifested or diagnosed and because television viewing at such young ages is controversial and discouraged," the researchers said.

The researchers controlled for a wide variety of potential confounders including sex; race or ethnicity; birth order; maternal use of alcohol, tobacco, or drugs during pregnancy; gestational age; maternal depression; and maternal self-esteem.

In all, the researchers obtained data on about 1,278 children at age 1 year and 1,345 children at age 3 years. The 1-year-olds watched an average of 2.2 hours of television per day; the 3-year-olds watched an average of 3.6 hours per day. Overall, 10% of the children had attentional problems by age 7 years. Every standard deviation increase in the number of television-viewing hours was associated with a 28% increase in the risk of attentional problems at age 7 years.

Limitations of the study

The study did have several important limitations. The first was that ADHD itself was not included in the analysis, although other studies have shown that results on the Behavior Problems Index correlate well with a subsequent diagnosis of ADHD, the authors wrote.

Also, researchers relied on parental reports of their children's television-viewing habits, which may not have always been accurate. And the findings say nothing about causal relationships: It's possible that children with attentional problems simply are drawn more than other children to the fast-paced entertainment on television. But the investigators tried to control for this possibility by focusing on TV viewing at 1 and 3 years of age, before the symptoms of ADHD manifest themselves.

It's also possible that parents who allow such young children to watch so much television may be more stressed, distracted, or neglectful than average, the researchers said. While they tried to account for as many variables as possible, "our analysis may have been imperfect." The study also did not address the content of the programs the children watched.

Television and attention spans

Nevertheless, these findings aren't surprising, because so many television programs present information in 15- to 20-second sound bites that require a very short attention span and could influence brain development in very young children, Dr. James Perrin, professor of pediatrics at Harvard Medical School, Boston, told this newspaper.

Children's interactions with other people, problem solving, and manipulation of their environments are the factors that permit optimal development of their nervous systems—not watching television, added Dr. Michael Rich, director of the Center on Media and Child Health at Children's Hospital, Boston.

It's for that reason that the American Academy of Pediatrics recommends that children watch no screen media at all before the age of 2, he said in an interview. Neither he nor Dr. Perrin were involved in this study.

Indeed, said Dr. Perrin, taking away the television could have a salutary effect, even on an older child.

"For children with a diagnosis of ADHD, improving the environment is one of the important treatment recommendations. That means the child needs to have quieter times, a place to get her homework done without distractions, and so on. I think that minimizing exposure to TV also would be helpful in managing a child's attentional problems, even if she's a little older," Dr. Perrin said.

But what's a clinician to say to harried parents who sometimes succumb to the convenience of using television as a babysitter?

> *Taking away the television could have a salutary effect, even on an older child.*

"Parents worked, parents cleaned the house, parents put dinner on the table for centuries before television was invented, so I think we have to be reminded that kids can do other things, such as playing with books or blocks or each other," Dr. Rich said.

Lazy parents, lazy kids

"I think we've gotten lazy about finding activities for kids, and kids have gotten lazy about looking for things to do other than just turning on the TV," he said.

Admittedly, it may take more effort to entertain a 1-year-old, Dr. Perrin said. "At that age it really does require an adult or older sibling to actually sit down next to the child and play with him. But that will pay off in the long run."

8

The Link Between Television and ADHD Is Unproven

Katy Read

Katy Read is a freelance writer living in Minneapolis.

The media have blown out of proportion a 2004 study linking television viewing with attention deficit/hyperactivity disorder (ADHD). That study did not provide clear evidence that television viewing causes the disorder. Much of the media coverage of the issue confuses causation with correlation. It is possible that instead of television viewing being a cause of ADHD, young children with ADHD-related problems are permitted by frazzled parents to watch more television. The experiences of many families call into question the tie between television viewing and ADHD.

I first heard about the study linking TV watching to attention-deficit (hyperactivity) disorder while, fittingly enough, watching TV. "Very scary," Katie Couric called it on NBC's "Today." Indeed. Something sank in my chest as Couric and a psychologist (not one involved in the research) discussed the implication that television can "rewire" the brains of young children and cause them to develop ADHD.

My first thought was, "Oh my God, I bet I've wrecked my kids."

My second thought was, "Oh my God, I bet they're confusing *correlation* with *causation* again."

Or so I assumed.

Not a smoking gun

The study itself, reported last month [April 2004] in the journal *Pediatrics*, hardly offers smoking-gun evidence that television causes brain damage. Researchers at the Children's Hospital and Regional Medical Center in Seattle examined massive, government-sponsored health surveys of more than a thousand children, conducted over the past 25 years, which asked parents (among other things) about their children's TV-viewing habits at ages 1 and 3, and then, four years later, whether their children were impulsive, obsessive, restless, easily confused or had difficulty concentrating. Turned out the more TV the kids reportedly watched as preschoolers, the more often they were described as having those behavioral problems at 7.

It's a finding worth looking into, no doubt, though it offers little reason to fear that a child who can sing the "Barney" song in nursery school will be on Ritalin by second grade. But that's the impression you might get from the newspapers and broadcasts. The media were not content to announce merely that an activity enjoyed in 98 percent of American homes, according to the Census Bureau, has been associated with a neurobiological disorder. Instead, when they reported on the study during the first week of April, they took the concept an alarming step further.

> *The study . . . hardly offers smoking-gun evidence that television causes brain damage.*

"Frequent TV-watching shortens kids' attention spans," blared a *USA Today* headline. "Researchers have found that every hour preschoolers watch television each day boosts their chances—by about 10 percent—of developing attention-deficit problems later in life," an Associated Press story warned. *Boston Globe* columnist Derrick Z. Jackson compared television to crack cocaine and equated its use with criminal child neglect, "now that we know that the passive babysitter we let into the house turned out to be a drug dealer, altering the brain perhaps even more permanently than a bag of dope."

Actually, we don't know that at all.

Even the study's authors, led by head researcher Dimitri A. Christakis, caution against drawing firm conclusions, though they do hypothesize along those lines. . . . ADHD experts I contacted agreed that the media blew the findings out of proportion. Some also questioned details of the study's design, though they differed on how much responsibility for the hyperbole belongs to its authors.

"I would say, based on the results of this study, that it would be worthwhile to look at this further. But I don't think this study can allow one to say, for example, that there's no safe level of TV viewing," said Linda Pfiffner, who directs a clinic for hyperactivity, attention and learning problems at the Langley Porter Psychiatric Hospital in San Francisco. "What parents need to understand is that most kids watch TV and most of them do not develop attention problems."

"It's easy to take a simplistic view of this study and draw some causal conclusion," said Jeff Epstein, director of Duke University Medical Center's ADHD program. "There are a lot of variables that could account for the relationship."

Confusing correlation with causation

Much of the media confusion seems to stem from a common error of logic: the faulty assumption that a *correlation* (in which levels of one thing, like TV, rise and fall in proportion to levels of another thing, like attention problems) means that the first thing *causes* the second.

Research on children is particularly vulnerable to this sort of misreading, said David B. Cohen, a psychologist and author of *Stranger in the Nest: Do Parents Really Shape Their Child's Personality, Intelligence or Character?*, partly because the interaction of genes and environment is so complicated. According to Cohen (based on research on twins and adopted children), correlations between kids' traits and their home environment are often not the result of their parents' behavior—contrary to conventional wisdom and the parenting-advice industry—but of inherited traits and other factors. In efforts to explain the connection between TV watching and attention problems, Cohen said, these other potential influences shouldn't be overlooked.

The Seattle researchers' method was valuable, ADHD experts noted, because it involved lots of kids observed over a long time. But because they were working with completed surveys, the researchers themselves acknowledged, they couldn't control what information was gathered. They didn't know, for example, whether the kids in the study spent their time watching "Sesame Street" or "Celebrities Uncensored." They had to take parents' word on both the children's behavior and their viewing habits (would a 1-year-old really sit still for five hours, Pfiffner wondered, riveted by a screen?). They didn't even know how many of the children actually *had* ADHD (the handful of behavioral problems they measured, Epstein pointed out, falls far short of an ADHD diagnosis). And although they attempted to adjust the figures to account for various aspects of the kids' home environments (emotional support, maternal self-esteem, etc.) they were limited to the available data and could not eliminate all other factors that might have affected the results.

> **[The study's finding] offers little reason to fear that a child who can sing the 'Barney' song in nursery school will be on Ritalin by second grade.**

To do that, you'd have to take a random bunch of kids, randomly assign them to watch TV or not, and see what happens. That's a complicated and expensive experiment—though one that, in light of these findings, might now attract funding, said lead researcher Christakis.

Christakis and his colleagues' results are "by no means definitive," he acknowledged in an interview. "But one has to keep in mind that it's a very important finding, particularly because it does have some biological plausibility."

He's referring to experiments done on rats in the 1980s, indicating that unusual types of visual stimulation can alter the physical structure of young animals' brains. Christakis and his fellow researchers hypothesized that early exposure to fast-moving television images might do something similar to children. If so, they speculated, those structural changes might contribute to attention problems.

But other factors also could explain the correlation they found—genes, for example. Scientists already know that ADHD is highly heritable. Parents who have it pass it on to their children; suppose those parents also are more likely to keep the TV turned on. The Seattle researchers couldn't rule that out.

"That was my first reaction when I was hearing about this

study: They didn't measure ADHD in the parents," Pfiffner said.

Another possibility is that the cause and effect might work in the other direction. Maybe ADHD "causes" TV viewing—that is, maybe small children with attention or hyperactivity problems are inclined (or allowed) to watch more television.

"ADHD kids can't sit quietly . . . maybe the parents just give in and say, 'OK, here's the TV, do what you want,'" Cohen said.

The study's authors wave away this interpretation, arguing that 1- and 3-year-olds are too young to display symptoms. But other experts weren't as quick to dismiss the idea that toddlers with ADHD could be more active and restless than their peers, even before their encounter with the rigid expectations of a classroom leads to a formal diagnosis.

"I don't find the rationale compelling that they're capturing kids before their risk has been established," Pfiffner said.

Family stories

Neither do I. My own two sons, now 8 and 9, do not have ADHD. But from their earliest years, the boys have been so extraordinarily rambunctious that life sometimes resembles one giant Halloween party. Early on, I developed a grudging appreciation for that smarmy purple dinosaur—or for any screen character who would keep them occupied long enough for me to get dinner prepared, the newspaper skimmed or a phone call made without having to wonder if the living-room curtains were being yanked off their rods.

Not that I was thrilled about relying on the dreaded "electronic babysitter." I once read a column by a mom who banned TV and boasted about her nonviolent, imaginative, nonmaterialistic kids. Her words echoed accusingly in my skull whenever one of my sons would grab a handful of the other's cheek and twist, or when they'd beg in the store for some new toy or candy they mysteriously knew all about. Exhausted, I would wonder how to turn them into the sort of kids who like to sit peacefully playing with blocks.

Eventually, I realized that I might as well have wished to change the color of their eyes (and, still later, understood that I didn't really want to fundamentally alter their personalities, anyway). Not long ago, author Daphne de Marneffe mentioned in a *Salon* interview that her children were so naturally easygoing that she could read whole novels while they played quietly at her feet. "A lot of how children are is temperament, a built-in thing," explained de Marneffe, a psychologist.

While my family's story doesn't prove anything, the experiences of other parents I spoke with don't necessarily support the research findings, either.

"My child was so hyperactive, he couldn't even watch TV until he went on medication," said Adrienne Nelson, who leads an ADHD support group in Chicago and whose son is now 17. She said she didn't believe what she heard about the study—especially because Nelson, 59, has the disorder herself. "For the first few years of my life, we didn't have a TV. And I was hyper and distracted. How do you explain that?"

Karran Harper Royal, 40, is skeptical about the study, too. Her 17-year-old was diagnosed with ADHD years ago, and her 8-year-old has shown signs of it and is being evaluated. But neither boy has ever watched much television. The New Orleans mother sharply restricted their viewing for reasons of her own.

"TV makes them relate too much to the television world instead of the real world," she said. "And I wanted my kids to be in the real world."

But some parents have trouble shrugging off what people in lab coats say. Having heard about the study, they may be morosely shouldering responsibility for their children's attention disorders. Like the "refrigerator mothers" who were blamed for their children's autism 50 years ago (incorrectly, it later developed), parents of children with developmental problems have often found themselves on the accusing end of psychologists' collective pointing finger.

> *What parents need to understand is that most kids watch TV and most of them do not develop attention problems.*

"The media puts us, parents with ADHD children, in a very negative light," read a posting on a message board for parents of kids with learning problems. "I am sure we'll be asked how much TV our kids watch, once someone knows that they have ADHD." A parent on another site moans, "I have grandparents now yelling at me saying I caused the (ADHD)."

Even parents whose kids *don't* have attention disorders may wonder whether there's reason for concern. Rewiring brains sounds awfully scary—what if all of the effects aren't immediately obvious? Some mothers and fathers might begin to question whether every C might, without TV, have been a B or an A. But Alison Gopnik, a psychologist and coauthor of *The Scientist in the Crib: What Early Learning Tells Us About the Mind*, warns that child development is way too complicated to reduce to a checklist of practices that determine whether a baby will "turn out fine . . . or be messed up."

Still, Gopnik doesn't see much harm in a little parental guilt. "Being a parent is the most profound moral responsibility anybody has. If you didn't feel guilty 90 percent of the time, you wouldn't be a moral person."

Anxious parents

These days, though, few parents complain of a shortage of things to worry about. Peter N. Stearns, author of *Anxious Parents: A History of Modern Childrearing in America*, says decades of alarming news stories and overblown research findings have sapped some of the joy out of family life.

"The experts are undoubtedly well-meaning—and also trying to get attention and funding," said Stearns, provost of George Mason University. "But the accumulation makes it very hard for parents to feel confident about what they're doing."

My questions about the new study's findings are not intended as a defense of television, or an argument that it's good for kids: For all I know, the idiot box is justly nicknamed. One can certainly imagine healthier pastimes for small children, activities that engage them in the three-dimensional world of human interaction and physical activity and all five senses. And sure, it's worth asking just what effect that flickering blue screen is having on malleable young minds. After all, that obnoxious purple dinosaur wasn't around during the millennia in which humankind did most of its evolving.

On the other hand, the record doesn't indicate how many of those Pleistocene-era parents emerged with their sanity—and their living-room curtains—intact.

9

Children with ADHD Should Not Be Seen as Handicapped

Thom Hartmann

Thom Hartmann is a psychotherapist and the author of The Edison Gene: ADHD and the Gift of the Hunter Child.

Attention deficit/hyperactivity disorder (ADHD) may have a genetic basis, but theories that people with ADHD are somehow "less evolved" must be rejected. People with ADHD should not be seen as flawed but instead as individuals who possess unique talents and creativity. The idea that ADHD is a "defect" must be resisted. Society should help ADHD children realize their potential rather than trying to drug them or force them into classroom and social conformity.

A distressing trend is emerging among a group I refer to as "neo-Darwinists," who imply or state flat-out that people with Attention Deficit/Hyperactivity Disorder (ADHD) are genetically dysfunctional, perhaps less evolved than "the rest of us," and thus have nothing to contribute to our culture whatsoever. Some have even called for ADHD adults to not have children, for fear that this "defect" will continue to spread. Others use the straw man scare tactic of threatening in professional publications that any discussion of ADHD that isn't purely "it's a genetic sickness" could lead to loss of funding for special education for ADHD children, or loss of profits to pharmaceutical manufacturers and practitioners who make their living working with ADHD children.

This trend is one that I believe is destructive to our children and dangerous to our society. Because many of these neo-Darwinists begin their work by either citing or condemning my work, I must respond on behalf of our children.

An explanatory metaphor

In the Seventies, when I was executive director of a residential treatment facility for disturbed children, I developed a metaphor to explain ADHD to children, a metaphor which I subsequently published in 1991. The metaphor was that hyperactive kids were actually "good hunters," whereas the very steady, stable, classroom-capable kids were "good farmers." The hunters, I suggested, would do great in the forest or battlefield: their constant scanning ("distractibility") would ensure they wouldn't miss anything; their ability to make instant decisions and to act on them ("impulsivity") would guarantee they'd be able to react to high-stress and response-demanding situations; and their love of stimulation ("need for high levels of stimulation") would cause them to enjoy the hunting world in the first place. (At its core, ADHD is diagnosed by evaluating the intensity and persistence of these three behaviors.) I told these kids, however, that they needed to learn the basic "farmer skills," because the world has been taken over by the farmers. Even our schools were organized by the farmers: schools let kids out in the summer so they can help bring in the crops. And factories and cubicles, of course, are just an industrial/technological age extension of the skill-set useful in agriculture.

The evidence that ADHD may be genetic, and my own experiences over the years visiting with indigenous agricultural and hunter/gatherer people on five continents, caused me to even think it possible that my metaphor might also prove to be "good science," although I have little certainty about whether it's genetics, culture, or both which so often causes indigenous people to fail when put into European-style classrooms. (I suspect both.)

Since the publication of this metaphor, I've presented it to tens of thousands of people at conferences on ADHD, neurology, and psychology from Australia to Israel to England to virtually every major city in the United States. During these lectures I suggested that perhaps in ancient times there was some sort of a "natural selection" process involved, to borrow a phrase from Darwin. I suggested that in hunting societies, those very risk-averse, super-methodical, check-it-five-times-before-doing-it people would not be particularly successful as hunters, and so would die off and not pass along their "farmer" genes. On the other hand, in the careful, stable farming societies (such as Japan over the past three thousand years), those wild and crazy hunter-types would be weeded out, executed, or expelled, and the culture would be left with a lot of very compliant followers and worker bees but few inventors, innovators, leaders, or—well—hunters.

I now realize that I should never, ever, have used a phrase invented by Darwin.

> *The banner of natural selection has now been picked up and twisted sideways to justify the worldview . . . that people with ADHD are suffering from a genetic defect.*

The banner of natural selection has now been picked up and twisted sideways to justify the worldview of some in the ADHD field that people with ADHD are suffering from a genetic defect. This defect, they say, is the result of evolution—which occasionally produces "more fit" and "less fit" members of a species. (Normally the "less fit" die out or are dominated by the "more fit," according to this interpretation of Darwin's work.) This is the natural course of the evolutionary process, they say, and the sometimes-explicit and sometimes-implicit message is that those with ADHD are less evolved, and that humans who do not have ADHD are more highly evolved, Darwinianly-speaking. . . .

What is superior?

The arrogance of the hypothesis that ADHD is an indicator of an evolutionary failure is breathtaking. . . . Such a hypothesis assumes that the narrowly defined criteria for success or failure in our particular culture at this particular point in time are identical to those of all cultures, all humans, and for all history, both past and future.

Cloaking themselves in the respectable mantle of science, the neo-Darwinists suggest that only in a rigorous application of the scientific method to the study of evolution will we find the ultimate answers to why people with ADHD appear to perform poorly compared with their non-ADHD peers. "Serious and scholarly evolutionary thinking about ADHD" is necessary, according to one . . . article in an ADHD publication, but must be constrained by an understanding of the "complexities of evolutionary theory" and "the processes of natural selection" for us to gain true insight into population genetics and whether a particular trait is adaptive or maladaptive. Nature is king, nurture is dead, and culture is irrelevant.

Even if the natural selection process with regard to the genetics of ADHD were true, the belief that ADHD represents a "defect" rests on a profoundly flawed assumption: that our culture and society are the pinnacle of an evolutionary process. This better/worse view of ADHD assumes the evolutionary process dictates that the "most fit" will be the survivors or, at the very least, the most prosperous, and that now is the endpoint time by which we must judge the fruits of natural selection. . . .

> *Too many psychologists . . . insist that people with ADHD can make little or no contribution to modern society.*

As Riane Eisler has so brilliantly documented in her book *The Chalice and the Blade*, a vast body of anthropological and archeological evidence points to human cultures and entire civilizations that were not exploitative, hierarchical, male-dominated, controlled by fear and power, or engaged in warfare. Indeed, today they are still here, represented by over 1,000 different indigenous societies in remote parts of the world. Only a tiny minority of these indigenous cultures engage in warfare or have hierarchical political structures: the vast majority are egalitarian, peaceful, and quite successful in their ways of life, those ways having sustained them for tens to hundreds of thousands of years.

In other words, there are different ways to live from the way in which we live. There are—and always have been different human cultures than our own. But, while older cultures value cooperation and security, our culture is set up to honor and support competition and domination—to feed resources to the most wealthy and powerful. Those people who are the most compliant and demur to authority figures are valued; they do not have "oppositional defiant disorder." Those people who can sit in a classroom for hours at a time, year after year, and then as adults sit in a cubicle or on an assembly line for hours at a time, year after year, are valued: they do not have "attention deficit hyperactive disorder." Those who have the ability to work easily and quickly with words and numbers are valued: they are not "retarded" and do not have "learning disabilities." Isn't it interesting that we have no diagnostic categories for "musically disordered," or "painting deficit disorder," or "creative thinking deficit"? These abilities do not produce good, compliant workers for our corporations and institutions, which are the leaders and definers of our culture. Therefore we don't even bother to measure or try to remedy deficiencies in them. . . .

As we move increasingly from the realm of difference to the realm of disorder, some physicians have now come forward to suggest that people with ADHD should be encouraged not to have children, lest their "genetic weaknesses" or lower evolutionary status be conferred on future generations. One such voice is Dr. David Comings. The thesis of his book, *The Gene Bomb*, is that people of "undesirable behavior" tend to have less education and to produce children at an earlier age (they are impulsive, after all) than well-educated persons, and therefore have more children. This produces a surplus of "undesirable" people, carrying "undesirable" genes, among our population. (In his writings, ADHD is explicitly deemed "undesirable."). . .

> *Few studies have looked for ADHD children who are functioning well in school, or ADHD adults who are functioning well in life.*

If only we could get rid of those rabble-rousers, the neo-Darwinists suggest, then the rest of us could have a civilized life! Get rid of those who couldn't make it in school (Thomas Edison was thrown out of school in the third grade, as was Ben Franklin); get rid of those who are incompetent at factory or office work (Vincent Van Gogh never held a job for more than two months); clear our gene pool of those who have no respect for legal authority (George Washington was sentenced to death by the King of England for treason). Then we would have an orderly society, an entire nation of third-little-pigs and well-built brick houses.

Too many psychologists, writing in respectable publications, insist that people with ADHD can make little or no contribution to modern society. They have called my farmer/hunter model a "Just So Story" after the fictional fables by Rudyard Kipling. These authors and others like them flatly state: "In not a single instance of peer-reviewed, published literature have symptoms or consequences of ADHD been found to hold an advantage."

Studies of ADHD children

There are several problems with this assertion. The first is the word "advantage." Of course, they mean "advantage" in the contemporary cultural context of a person's ability to function in a public school or work in a factory or office cubicle. In fact, virtually all the studies that have been published in the peer-reviewed literature of psychology are looking at the ability of an ADHD child to function in a "boring/farmer" environment, as this is what society rewards and so is our current criterion for "good." Failure in this arena makes one a potential customer for the drug companies that fund such research. Few studies have ever bothered to test ADHD kids against "normal" children on, for example, their ability to outscore in one of the new, high-stimulation video games or outperform on a skateboard . . . yet we all know how brilliantly these "impaired" children can function in these "non-useful" areas. In the real world, if these children could survive the experience of public school, such behaviors could translate into being a competent air traffic controller or a successful entrepreneur.

Since all the studies are looking for "impairment" in a specific and narrowly circumscribed range of capabilities, it should surprise none of us that most find impairment—particularly since the children being tested were identified as having ADHD by virtue of that "boredom impairment" in the first place (by their teachers or parents, who then referred them for testing and/or medication). In a letter to the editor of *Scientific American* magazine, psychologist Russell A. Barkley says, "Some studies have shown that ADHD can reduce IQ scores by an average of seven to 10 points." Of course, what the writer overlooks is the fact that the first thing an IQ test tests is the ability of a person to take a test: this, in and of itself, does not necessarily indicate intelligence unless one defines "intelligence" as meaning only the ability to take tests and perform in contemporary public school environments.

Few studies have looked for ADHD children who are functioning well in school, or ADHD adults who are functioning well in life (although we all know of examples of the latter, from actors to entrepreneurs to inventors to artists). Because publications of the psychology and psychiatry industries concern themselves only with pathology (there is no listing for "normal" in the Diagnostic and Statistical Manual of Mental Disorders of the American Psychiatric Association, for example), it should not surprise us that they find it. Nor should it surprise us that they wouldn't bother to look for or at those who are not "failing" in society, and thus not potential customers.

Thus, people like multi-millionaire entrepreneur Wilson Harrell (former publisher of *Inc.* magazine and founder of the Formula 409 company) are completely overlooked. Harrell, in his book *For Entrepreneurs Only*, devotes two chapters to his own ADHD and his belief that ADHD is "essential" for the success of an entrepreneur. Similarly, those who don't care to look for ADHD among the ranks of the successful would overlook Harvard psychiatrists and professors of psychiatry Drs. John Ratey and Edward Hallowell, authors of the best-selling book *Driven to Distraction*, in which they state explicitly that they each "have ADD."

> **❝** *ADHD children look much more like a symptom of a society which itself may be severely dysfunctional.* **❞**

In fact, several studies have provided us with hints that ADHD may be useful somehow, somewhere, sometime. One of the most interesting was a Washington University study in which ADHD persons were tested against "normal" controls for their ability to handle emergencies, what the study's authors called "urgent tasks." The abstract reads:

> Attention-deficit hyperactivity disorder (ADHD) has been proposed to represent adaptive responding to highly urgent situations in primitive hunt-

ing. In the present study, 31 adults with self-reported ADHD were compared with 33 normal adults on a newly developed, 10-item measure of urgent task involvement. The internal consistency of the scale was suitable, and the group with ADHD scored significantly higher than the control group, as predicted.

While this was the first study to demonstrate that people with ADHD had some advantage in some circumstances over others, many previous studies offer tantalizing glimpses which the researchers chose not to pursue. For example, one study found that while "normal" children's ability to read or perform tasks requiring vigilance deteriorated when they were "distracted" by high levels of external stimulation, ADHD children's scores actually improved. Another study found that boys with ADHD calmed down when they were in highly stimulating environments, whereas "normal" children would crash and burn under such circumstances. An article in *The Journal of Creative Behavior* by University of Georgia's Bonnie Cramond asks the question in its abstract: "There are so many similarities in the behavioral descriptions of creativity and ADHD that one is left to wonder, could these be overlapping phenomena?" The article goes on to suggest that a thorough search of the literature in both fields would imply the answer is yes. It concludes:

> Perhaps individuals who have trouble with verbal learning but have a very imaginative, visual manner of thinking will be considered at the forefront of innovation in our society rather than as problem learners. Taken together, the results of these studies and others like them are indicative of a childhood syndrome characterized by hyperactivity and high intelligence, in which personality variables, modes of cognitive representation and creativity are intimately bound.

A dysfunctional society

Instead of trying to rid ourselves of ADHD children, our society would be far better served were we to ask, "How can we acknowledge and honor the individuality of each of our children, and provide settings in which each can develop into a happy, effective, and caring adult?" Were we to provide education that acknowledges the differences in the way people learn, we might soon be tapping a source of creativity that could be useful to our entire society. But to do that would require that we open ourselves up to the possibility that the kinds of skills we reward today may not be the only worthwhile skills—and that would open the question of whether the way we organized our society itself was the only or best way to create a society.

When such questions are on the agenda, ADHD children look much more like a symptom of a society which itself may be severely dysfunctional. If we cannot find the tools to reorganize our world immediately, we at least ought to do what we can to prevent educational and eugenic philosophies that seek to denigrate the beings of those who do not fit into this distorted reality.

10

The Forced Drugging of Students Diagnosed with ADHD Is a Serious Problem

William Norman Grigg

William Norman Grigg is senior editor for the New American, *a magazine published by the John Birch Society.*

Some public school officials are diagnosing children with attention deficit/hyperactivity disorder (ADHD) and threatening parents with child abuse or neglect charges if they refuse to medicate these children with Ritalin or other drugs. Children are being diagnosed for simply being disruptive in class, many parents believe. Tragically, some children have died from drug complications from ADHD medications that may have been unnecessary.

Shaina Dunkle was a bright, energetic 10-year-old girl when she died in a pediatrician's office in Bradford, Pennsylvania, in February 2001. A little more than a half-hour earlier, she had collapsed in the school library. Shaina had asthma and problems with her kidneys and urinary tract, but these problems weren't responsible for her tragic and unexpected death. A postmortem ruled that the child died from the toxic effects of Desipramine, a psychoactive drug she had been compelled to take after a school psychiatrist suggested she suffered from Attention Deficit Hyperactivity Disorder (ADHD).

William Norman Grigg, "Drugging Our Kids," *The New American*, vol. 19, August 25, 2003. Copyright © 2003 by American Opinion Publishing Incorporated. Reproduced by permission.

Shaina's story

Shaina's problems began while attending first grade in 1997. Like many other normal and healthy youngsters, she had problems sitting still, concentrating on classroom instructions, and listening to her teachers. In an interview with the investigative radio program *Scams & Scandals*, Shaina's mother Vicky recalled that the youngster "was placed outside the classroom [and] not allowed to study with the other children." On one occasion, Shaina's teacher, rebuking the child for having a messy desk, emptied its contents on the classroom floor and had her replace them as her classmates erupted in laughter. Old enough to feel the sting of ostracism, Shaina started to have "nightmares [and was] beginning to be afraid of going to school" Vicky related to her radio audience.

Knowing that their daughter had challenges with learning that could only be addressed on a one-to-one basis, Vicky and her husband Steve took Shaina out of class and home-schooled her for the rest of her first grade year. "I could see a definite difference in her behavior, and she was making very good progress in her studies," Vicky told *The New American*. As the summer of 1998 waned and children prepared to return to school, Shaina—feeling the pull of peer group—wanted to go back. "She saw the other girls her age getting their school clothes and backpacks, and she wanted to be with them," Vicky recalled. After consulting with school officials, Vicky and Steve relented. But within the first two weeks of classes, Shaina's problems resumed.

> *Steve and Vicky plausibly contend that the school officials who insisted on drugging Shaina were directly responsible for her . . . death.*

"Shaina was behind the other children," Vicky recounted. "We wanted to have her undergo a learning support evaluation." Immediately after that evaluation—in January 1999, halfway through the school year—Shaina was placed in a learning support program. But this didn't satisfy school officials. "In March [1999]," Vicky recalled, "we got a letter from the school psychologist telling us that Shaina was still struggling, and that she displayed all of the 'characteristics' of a child suffering from Attention Deficit Hyperactivity Disorder. This seemed odd to us, because Shaina wasn't a disciplinary problem for anybody. She was an obedient child, sweet, caring, and giving. She did have a short attention span, and could be distracted fairly easily, but these are hardly abnormal traits in a child her age. And she did have challenges to overcome in her schoolwork. But the psychologist and other school officials focused on ADHD as the problem, and began pressuring us—not forcing us, but pressuring us—to have her examined and 'medicated.'"

Although they balked at the suggestion, Vicky continued, "we were beginning to believe that something must be wrong. After all, we thought, these people are the experts. They're with these children eight hours a day. If this is what they say needs to be done, maybe we should do it." In April 1999, the Dunkles visited a physician. Forty-five minutes later they emerged with a diagnosis of ADHD and a prescription for Wellbutrin.

> *Many parents have discovered that refusing to drug their children may be met with child abuse or neglect charges and the loss of their parental rights.*

Almost immediately the side effects became visible: Shaina began to lose weight and her disposition changed. Vicky took Shaina off the drug and took her back to the physician, who prescribed another drug called Effexor, which led to recurring bouts of insomnia. After the third visit, the second grader was put on a third drug, Desipramine, "which we were told had fewer side effects and was less likely to be abused than Ritalin," Vicky observed.

At first, "Shaina seemed to respond well to the Desipramine," Vicky continued. "Her attention span got longer, her handwriting got neater. But then we got calls from the school telling us that she was relapsing. This happened several times, and each time we took her back for treatment—which meant a larger dose of Desipramine." Neither Shaina nor her parents were warned that Desipramine (which the FDA [Food and Drug Administration] has not approved) should not be used by people suffering from kidney ailments, as Shaina did.

After starting with a daily dosage of 10 milligrams, Shaina's daily intake steadily increased to 200 milligrams by February

2001—and her physical and behavioral problems escalated as well. Shortly before she died, "Shaina acted out in class, throwing a pencil at one student and threatening another with scissors," Vicky told *The New American.* "This sent up vivid red flags for her teachers, and for us, too, because Shaina was never an aggressive or violent child."

In mid-February 2001, Shaina's physician—who insisted that Desipramine wasn't causing the side effects—ramped up the daily dose to 250 milligrams. One week later, Shaina was dead.

"That morning, I gave her breakfast, French-braided her hair, and then administered her 250 milligrams of that drug," Vicky recalled to *The New American.* "She left at a quarter to eight, saying, 'I'll see you at three, Mommy.'" Three hours later Vicky got a call from the school nurse saying that Shaina had fallen and injured her cheek during what appeared to be a mild seizure. Vicky and Steve rushed to the school, collected their child, and drove her to the doctor's office.

> *If I had known about the risks and effects of those drugs, there is no way I would have allowed them to drug my son.*

Shaina appeared normal during the half-hour drive. As Vicky signed in with the receptionist, Shaina collapsed into a seizure. A physician rushed in to examine the child; after a moment he instructed a nurse to "call a code 99." "I've worked in hospitals, and I knew that 'code 99' referred to cardiac arrest," Vicky explained. "Shaina looked into my eyes as her life ended, and I could do nothing to save her," recalled Vicky. "It's been two and a half years, and I relive those last few minutes every day."

The coroner's report certified that Shaina was killed by Desipramine toxicity. As her dosage increased—in response to complaints from school officials that her behavior wasn't improving—Shaina was unable to metabolize the drug. The accumulated toxins in her bloodstream precipitated a heart attack.

Vicky and Steve adopted Shaina at birth. Vicky was present in the delivery room when Shaina took her first breath and present in the pediatrician's office when she took her last. "I believe God sent her to us to take care of," commented Vicky, "and I've asked God too many times to count why He took her from us." Every single night, Vicky and Steve visit a nearby cemetery to pray over Shaina's grave.

Just say no?

Steve and Vicky plausibly contend that the school officials who insisted on drugging Shaina were directly responsible for her tragic and unnecessary death. "Children go to school to be educated, not medicated," stated Vicky Dunkle. "Parents should not be pressured to drug their children."

Over the past decade, the federal government has spent millions of dollars on drug prevention programs targeting school-age youth. At the insistence of the federal Office of National Drug Control Policy, counter-narcotics messages have been insinuated into youth-oriented television programs. With the help of federal subsidies, Drug Abuse Resistance Education (DARE) programs have been set up in nearly every school system across the country. But at the same time, school officials nationwide routinely insist that children said to suffer from ADHD be placed on various psychoactive drugs, particularly Ritalin—listed by the FDA as a Class II controlled substance along with opium, codeine, morphine, and cocaine.

Much of the counter-narcotics propaganda generated by the Office of National Drug Control Policy focuses on the stereotypical schoolyard drug pusher, usually portrayed as a grimy adult or a bullying older youth. Anti-drug messages extol open communication between parents and children, and urge children to stand up boldly to pushers.

All of this is well and good, of course. But, asks *Scams & Scandals* host/investigator Tai Aguirre, what if "the drug pusher happens to be your school social worker or psychologist, and they're telling you your child either takes their drugs or they won't be allowed in school—or, even worse, that [they're] going to charge you, the parent, with neglect? What do you do then? Do you 'just say no'? *Can* you say no?"

Drug him—or lose him

Speaking at a congressional hearing in August 2002, Neil Bush—brother of President George W. Bush—described his own seven-year ordeal when his son Pierce was diagnosed with ADHD at age 10. "There is a systematic problem in this country, where schools are often forcing parents to turn to Ritalin," concluded Bush. "It's obvious to me we have a crisis in this country."

Many parents have discovered that refusing to drug their children may be met with child abuse or neglect charges and the loss of their parental rights. This highlights a critical difference between street-corner drug pushers and their counterparts on the government's payroll. A private pusher can't force children to take drugs by telling them that they will otherwise be torn from their families.

> *Advocates for the forced medication of schoolchildren diagnosed with ADHD and similar dubious maladies are unapologetic about the use of such totalitarian methods.*

In July 2000, Michael and Jill Carroll of Albany, New York, were reported to social services authorities after they took their son Kyle off Ritalin. As is the case with many other youngsters on Ritalin, Kyle displayed a loss of appetite and difficulty sleeping.

When Mr. and Mrs. Carroll decided that it would be in Kyle's best interest to stop using the drug, an official from the local school district filed a complaint with Albany County's Department of Social Services. A family court judge ruled that the parents must continue to drug their son to avoid child abuse charges. In a story on the case, Albany's NBC affiliate WNYT-TV reported that "Social Service workers will visit the family throughout the next year" to assure that the parents comply.

This highlights another distinction between government dope-pushers and their private-sector equivalents: Private pushers are content to sell their product; they don't thrust their way into their customers' homes and force them to consume it.

The Carrolls are hardly the first or only parents forced to dope their children under the threat of losing them. In 2000, Patricia Weathers of Millbrook, New York, was "hot-lined" by local school officials—threatened with the seizure of her son by Child Protective Services—after she took him off a drug regimen that included Ritalin, Dextrostat, and Paxil.

"When Michael was in kindergarten and first grade, his teachers told me he had behavior problems—he was easily distracted, had problems focusing, and wouldn't sit down," Patricia told *The New American*. "I was told that if I didn't 'medicate' him—that is, drug him—he wouldn't learn. I was assured that the drugs were mild. I wasn't told that they are as dangerous as cocaine, or that there were health risks and side effects. They kept calling me down to the office, wearing me down. Eventually the principal told me point-blank: 'Counseling is too slow. Think of medicating this child or I will do everything in my power to transfer him into a special education program.' So we started him on Ritalin just before the end of his first grade year."

According to Patricia, Michael was "diagnosed" with ADHD on the basis of the Acters Profile for Boys, a widely used checklist for behavior disorders. "It basically lists stereotypical boy behaviors—untidiness, disorganization, inattentiveness—as symptoms of ADHD," she contended. School officials just "checked off the list, gave it to the pediatrician, and he put Michael on Ritalin." Significantly, Patricia observed, "I only put him on the drugs when he was going to school. He never had it on weekends, or on summer vacation. And I would never have done this if it weren't for the coercion from the school."

From healthy to haunted

By third grade, Michael's behavior had deteriorated dramatically. "He was eating his clothing, slobbering, and did not want to go out for recess," related Patricia. Michael was put on Dextrostat, which apparently exacerbated his problems. Rather than reconsidering the wisdom of drugging the child, school officials insisted that Michael suffered from "some other disorder"—variously described as either bi-polar disorder or "social anxiety." Paxil, an anti-anxiety drug—was added to the regimen.

By this time—late 1999—"Michael was telling me, 'Mom, it makes me feel bad,'" Patricia told *The New American*. "He was having major incidents of violent behavior, hallucinating, and even hearing voices. I finally took him off the drugs in October 1999, and started doing my own research." After learning of the drugs' side effects and health risks, Patricia confronted school officials in early January. "I made it very clear that we were finished with the drug route," she recalled. "The principal slammed my information down on my desk and said, 'We have nothing left to offer Michael.'"

Shortly thereafter, as Patricia prepared to fly to Texas with her son to seek specialized medical treatment, she was informed that school officials had "hot-lined" her to Child Protective Services (CPS), claiming that she was guilty of medical neglect. "[Michael's] behavior at school is bizarre: He hears voices and appears delusional, he chews on his clothes and paper, he talks to himself and rambles when he talks," stated the child abuse complaint filed against Patricia Weathers by the local school district. A month-long investigation cleared Patricia of child abuse and "medical neglect" after evaluations by independent psychiatrists proved that Michael's symptoms reflected state-ordered drug use, rather than parental mistreatment.

"I trusted the judgment of 'experts' rather than my own common sense," commented Patricia to *The New American*. "Millions of other parents make the same mistake. If I had known about the risks and effects of those drugs, there is no way I would have allowed them to drug my son." While Patricia Weathers and her son survived both the forced drugging and the attempted child grab, six months after Michael was taken off the drugs he was found to have a heart murmur—a recognizable, if rare, side effect of drugs like Ritalin.

Michael has been home-schooled for three years, and may enroll in private school this fall. "It's wonderful," Patricia enthused. "It was difficult at first, but he's growing and thriving now—and he loves to learn. He was socially isolated while he was on the drugs, and now he's anxious to socialize and play sports."

A tragic case

Fourteen-year-old Matthew Smith of Auburn Hills, Michigan, was not so fortunate. He died on March 21, 2000, after seven years of state-imposed Ritalin use. Matthew's death certificate candidly states: "Death caused from long term use of methylphenidate [Ritalin]." Dr. Ljuba Dragovic, a pathologist who presided over Matthew's autopsy, noted that the youngster's heart displayed tell-tale small vessel damage from prolonged Ritalin use. (At the time of death Matthew's heart had swollen to 402 grams—larger than that of a full-grown man, which typically weighs 350 grams.)

"We were told Matt had ADHD when he was six years old," Matt's father Larry told *The New American*. "We were told that the condition was a legitimate medical disorder, that he needed the Ritalin in order to deal with this objective medical condition. But we just didn't have a good feeling about putting our boy on drugs." As Matt's parents dragged their feet, the pressure to drug their child increased. A letter from the school social worker to Matthew's parents complained: "We would have hoped you would have started Matthew on a trial of medication by now." At one counseling session, Larry Smith recounted to *The New American*, "the social worker told us we could be charged with medical or emotional neglect if we refused to take Matthew to the doctor and get him on Ritalin. My wife and I were intimidated and scared. We believed that there was a very real possibility of losing our children if we did not comply with the school's threats."

The Smiths took Matthew to see a physician in Birmingham, Michigan. On the basis of what Larry calls "a five-minute pencil twirling trick," Matthew was diagnosed as having ADHD. As the physician scribbled out a prescription for Ritalin, he "asked us to remind the school that he was not a pharmacy," recalled Larry Smith. "I can only conclude from his comment that we were not the first parents sent to him by this school."

Essentially, the school system used the implied threat of kidnapping the Smiths' children to force them to drug their oldest, which resulted in his death.

A growing scourge

Forced drugging of schoolchildren has become so common that the mainstream press—which can usually be counted on to carry water for the government school system—has taken note. *USA Today* for August 8, 2000, reported that "some public schools are accusing parents of child abuse when they balk at giving their kids drugs such as Ritalin, and as judges begin to agree, some parents are medicating their children for fear of having them hauled away."

Advocates for the forced medication of schoolchildren diagnosed with ADHD and similar dubious maladies are unapologetic about the use of such totalitarian methods. "It's becoming increasingly clear that this is a powerful treatment that can be life-saving for some children," insists Peter Jensen, a board member of Children and Adults with Attention Deficit Disorder (CHADD), which advocates the use of Ritalin and similar drugs. "This is going to be happening more and more," he promises.

Dr. Jensen, whose high-profile advocacy earned him the sobriquet "Mr. ADHD," does believe, however, that there are a few parents whose judgement can be trusted when they refuse to drug their children. Speaking at a gathering of psychologists in December 2001, Dr. Jensen emphasized that "medication is not the only effective nor . . . the best treatment option for every child," reported the *Monitor on Psychology.* "When his own child was diagnosed with ADHD," Jensen told the audience, "he and his wife opted not to use medication."

11

Medication Can Help Children with Attention Deficit Disorder

Amy Wojtkielewicz

Amy Wojtkielewicz was an eighth grader at Walnut Creek School in Erie, Pennsylvania, at the time this article was first published.

People with attention deficit disorder (ADD) are normal people who should make the choice to not let the disorder control their lives. They should take the medication prescribed to control the disorder and agree to counseling. Medication is especially important because it helps people with ADD to control their moods.

My name is Amy. I am a 15-year-old girl from Erie, Pennsylvania, and I have attention deficit disorder (ADD). Part of my treatment is working with Jennifer Girts, a counselor at the Achievement Center near my home. One afternoon when I was really frustrated, she gave me an article on ADD and adolescents. Wow! I loved it! It really helped me understand a lot about myself. Now I feel moved to write my own article telling my story: when I was diagnosed, the ways I felt about it then, and how I am coping now. Having dealt with ADD for nine years, I know how other kids with it feel. I was there at one time, too, and I hope my story will help.

Before we found out about ADD, my childhood was good. I have wonderful parents and a younger brother, Brian, who mean the world to me. I was good and bad, just like any other

Amy Wojtkielewicz, "My Choice for My Life: Coming to Terms with ADD," *Exceptional Parent*, vol. 30, November 2000. Copyright © 2000 by *Exceptional Parent*. Reproduced by permission.

child. Then, in first grade, we found out I have ADD. My life changed from then on.

My parents had taken me to all different kinds of counselors because I had trouble paying attention in school and would lose my temper all the time. Sometimes I would be mad at my family for no reason—especially on school nights. I would pack my book bag and stomp out the front door. I remember one time when I was really angry and acting out, I walked out and my parents actually locked me out! I screamed really loud because I was really scared. Brian was very upset. I was only 6 years old! I can look back now and laugh. Over the years, I would do this kind of stuff to my parents. But they never gave up on me. They were always there for me when I needed them.

Coming to terms with ADD

When I first heard about ADD, I did not know what it was. I remember asking my parents about it. They explained it to me and I asked, "Will it ever go away?" The answer: "No." This made me really upset. They assured me that ADD could be treated, but that I needed to want the help.

I was more than halfway through the first grade when we found out about my ADD. My parents made the decision to hold me back because of all the trouble I was having in school. To this day, I can remember the pain I felt when they told me I was going to repeat first grade. I was mad when they told me, and for a long time afterwards! Especially when school started again. I was always made fun of because I was older than the rest of the kids. I still get upset about being held back, and now and then, want to blame it on my parents. Sometimes I feel, "How could you do this to me? I thought you loved me. I hate you." Luckily, my family was always there for me. I don't know where I would be if they had ever given up on me.

> *I finally realized that I need the medication to help myself.*

Today, I realize that even if you have ADD, it doesn't make you different from anyone else. We are all people and we all matter in this world. Please, do not let anyone tell you different. If they do, don't believe them. I know what you are going through because I was once there myself or I still am. We are all the same: people who need love and understanding.

> **❝ ADD may never go away, but I have the power to control it. ❞**

My parents thought bringing me to a psychiatrist, who could give me medication, would help me. I thought I was going to lose my head trying all the different kinds of medications suggested. I ended up trying eight different kinds. Can you believe it? I took kinds that made me less hungry, some that made me depressed, and others that made me confused. Finally, my doctor found a combination that works. Now I am on Adderall and Clonidine.

Making a choice

Finally we found the right medication, but then I never wanted to take it. I would hide it in my dog's chew toys or put it up my sleeve. Now I find myself wondering why I would want to do that since the medication really does help me. My mom assures me there was a time when I didn't care if it did or not. Here is the real reason: I wanted to be normal. After all, no other kid I knew took medication. But when I did not take my medication, I always had difficulty paying attention, and my grades dropped. I was a grouch—definitely not a nice person—all because I did not take my medication.

Finally, my counselor said to me, "Amy, it is your choice to take your medication or not. A lot of people take medication for all different kinds of reasons. You need to decide if you want to be in control of your moods and impulsivity. What kind of person do you want to be: someone in control or a grouch?" I finally realized that I need the medication to help myself. That's the way my father put it. He would say, "You need to help yourself before you can help others."

Listen, it's up to you. It's your choice; no one can force you to take your medicine. I know which person I would rather be. It was up to me to make the right choice—not my parents or my counselor. Other people can ask me to take medication, but

I need to be smart enough to realize that I need it. I found out that it was the best thing for me. So my advice to others is: be smart and take your medication. It will help you—take my word for it.

Now my life is pretty good. I am in the eighth grade. I make good grades and have tons of friends. I still take my medication every morning and at night. And I still see my counselor every once in a while. She helps me sort out my feelings and ask myself the right questions. But, hey, I have ADD. And I am normal.

Don't get me wrong, I still have my ups and downs—everyone does. It's not because of ADD; it's because I am human. My life has changed over the years. I've come to understand what ADD can mean to me. ADD may never go away, but I have the power to control it. I will not let it control me again. I have made my choice. The right choice. You have to decide how you want to live: as Oscar the Grouch, or as a person in control with a wonderful life. What is your choice?

12

Alternatives to Drug Treatment of ADHD Should Be Pursued

Farhang Khosh and Deena Beneda

Farhang Khosh and Deena Beneda are both practicing physicians with degrees in naturopathic medicine—the treatment of disease using natural products such as herbs and minerals, as well as through exercise, diet, and therapies such as acupuncture.

Conventional medicine has had limited success in dealing with attention deficit/hyperactivity disorder (ADHD). Ritalin and other drugs used to treat this disorder have many undesired side effects, such as weight loss and psychiatric problems. Alternative medicine—including nutrition therapies, herbs, and homeopathy—could effectively treat ADHD without side effects, and should be encouraged for children diagnosed with ADHD.

Attention Deficient Hyperactive Disorder or better known as ADHD, is becoming more common in children throughout the United States. It is reaching epidemic portions and yet few advancements have been done to effectively treat, manage or eliminate ADHD. Current treatment relies on pharmaceutical drugs, which not only do not eliminate the condition but have both short and long-term side effects. Alternative therapies focus on nutrition, vitamins and minerals, amino acids, herbs, homeopathy, food and environmental allergies, and proanthocyanidins. In addition, hypothyroidism and adrenal glands have also been mentioned in the literature in relation to ADHD. An integrative alternative approach should be considered in the treatment and management of ADHD.

The term ADHD was originally derived from the term ADD (attention deficit disorder). ADD was further subcategorized as ADD with hyperactivity or ADD without hyperactivity. However, in the 1994 *DSM-IV* [*Diagnostic and Statistical Manual of Mental Disorders-Fourth Edition*] the official term was stated as ADHD.

A child with ADHD has a wide range of symptoms including hyperactivity, short attention span, distractibility, and difficulty with organizational skills and not paying attention to details. These children are restless, forgetful and react impulsively. They may have mood swings, temper tantrums and are unable to cope with stress. Boys seem to be two to three times more likely to be diagnosed with ADHD. Some of the current research examines the possibility that ADHD is inherited. Twin and adoption studies suggest that ADHD has a relatively high degree of hereditability. However, to date there is insufficient data linking ADHD to an inherited trait.

In order to diagnose a child with ADHD the behaviors must appear before age seven and be present at a minimum of six months. ADHD occurs in 3% to 5% of children in the United States, and approximately half of those children continue to have ADHD symptoms as adults. Those that continue to have symptoms into adulthood may develop antisocial behavior, substance abuse, suffer from poor self-esteem and social skill deficits. In 1993, more than two million children were diagnosed with ADHD; this was an increase from 902,000 in 1990. It is estimated that as many as four million children currently have been diagnosed with ADHD.

Conventional ADHD drugs

Currently, conventional medical interventions include pharmaceutical drugs. Psychostimulants are the first line of defense used in ADHD. Methylphenidate or Ritalin is the most common drug prescribed to treat ADHD. In 1993, more than 2.5 million prescriptions were written for Ritalin. Other stimulants that can be used are dextroamphetamine (Dexedrine), a mixture of four salts of dextroamphetamine (Adderall), methamphetamine (Desoxyn) or pemoline (Cylert). Ritalin and Ritalin-SR are preparations of mythyl-alpha-phenyl-2-piperidineacetate hydrochloride. Ritalin acts on the central nervous system with a dopamine-agonistic effect that works slower but is mechanically almost identical to cocaine and amphetamines. Most all of the mood altering drugs (alcohol, cigarettes, caffeine, heroin, cocaine, and the stimulant medications for hyperactive children) affect dopamine.

Research has found that ADHD children have a deficiency in dopamine, a chemical in the brain necessary for several vital brain functions. The dopamine system is involved in the reward-seek behavior, sexual behavior, control of movements, regulation of the pituitary-hormone secretion and memory functions. Dopamine has been shown in young animals to exert a protective influence against hyperactivity. It is thought ADHD children have too many molecules that use up the dopamine before it can be used for its vital functions. Ritalin binds to these molecules allowing the dopamine levels to increase in the brain and be used for the normal vital functions.

> *Pharmaceutical drugs . . . not only do not eliminate the condition but have both short and long-term side effects.*

Even though Ritalin is the drug of choice for children with ADHD, it has many side effects and presents many risks for the children who use it. A child who is treated with Ritalin is moved from a hyperactive state to the opposite state. Children develop appetite suppression, weight loss, retarded growth, emotional blunting and detachment, and many parents complain that the child acts like a "zombie." Children on higher doses and chronic use may develop paranoid symptoms—withdrawal, anger, restlessness, and suspicious behavior. It has been shown that adults who abuse amphetamines regularly develop psychotic states with paranoid features. Other serious side effects of methylphenidate are auditory and visual hallucinations, drug abuse–rebound depression, psychic dependence, increased euphoria and cocaine-like activity, insomnia and tachycardia. Also, researchers reported that Ritalin caused liver cancer in mice. No drug that affects the dopamine system is free of long-term toxicity to the motor system. Ritalin may produce disruption of movement control and facial and head tics may appear. Amphetamines are commonly referred to as "speed or uppers" and are one of the most dangerous medications ever discovered. They are chemically similar to dopamine and are the synthetic replacement in the dopamine receptor sites of the brain. Amphetamines have the potential to cause injury to healthy tissue, interfere with growth and development, sleep problems, or aggressive and depressed moods in children.

How can we increase dopamine levels in children with ADHD naturally without using Ritalin or other amphetamines? Dopamine is made from the amino acids tyrosine, or phenylalanine. These amino acids are converted by enzymes into L-dopa. Folic acid, niacin and iron are required for the enzyme to make L-dopa from tyrosine. Finally, another enzyme converts L-dopa to dopamine as long as vitamin B6 is available. By supplementing nutrients and amino acids the body can make dopamine naturally, increasing its levels in the brain. In addition, one study examined the plasma amino acids in 28 patients diagnosed with ADD and 20 control subjects. Compared to the controls, the ADD subjects had significantly lower levels of phenylalanine, tyrosine, tryptophan, histidine, and isoleucine. This suggests there may be a general deficiency in amino acid transport, absorption or both in ADD. . . .

Much has been said in the literature relating diet to ADHD. Dietary influences such as food and environmental allergies and nutritional deficiencies have been linked to hyperactivity. By focusing on nutrition, proanthocyanidins, essential fatty acids, supplementing with vitamins/minerals, and eliminating allergens have been very effective in treating ADHD.

Food allergies

Food allergies and food chemistry are important in causing learning and behavior problems in children. When children are sick or influenced by food and/or airborne chemicals it can compromise brain function. Their learning is impaired and behavior may be disturbed. Feingold research found that up to 50% of all hyperactive children were sensitive in food additives (artificial food colors, flavorings and preservatives) plus salicylates occurring naturally in some foods, making the connection between food allergies and hyperactivity. Since then research has made the connection with foods and ADHD. Seventy-eight children with hyperactivity behavior were placed on an elimination diet. Fifty-nine (76%) of the children improved in behavior. These 59 children who responded were then challenged with various foods and some food additives. It was found the additive containing foods were the worst offenders (70% reacted). Then the list was as follows: chocolate (64%), cow's milk (64%), orange (57%), cow's cheese (45%), wheat (45%), other fruits (35%), tomato (22%) and egg (18%). Another study with 26 children who met the criteria for ADHD were put on a multiple item elimination diet and showed 19 children responding favorably and with an open challenge all 19 children reacted to many foods, dyes and/or preservatives. This study shows the benefit of eliminating reactive foods and artificial colors in the diets of children with ADHD. Finally, a study involving 40 children who were given a diet free of artificial food dyes and other additives for five days; 20 of the children were classified as hyperactive and the other 20 were controls without a hyperactive classification. On oral challenges with food dyes the performance of the hyperactive children was impaired relative to their performance after receiving the placebo. The performance of the nonhyperactive group was not affected by the challenge of the food dyes. The United States consumes an enormous amount of food additives. Per capita daily consumption of food additives is 13–15 grams, and the population's total annual consumption of food colors alone is approximately 100 million pounds. There are some 5,000 additives currently is widespread use. Other countries have significantly restricted artificial food additives. The removal of artificial food colorings and preservatives from the diet of a child with ADHD is vital and a realistic clinical intervention.

Environmental illness can play an important role in ADHD. Environmental toxins include everything from molds, dust, and pollens to toxic chemicals (pesticides, herbicides, solvents, etc.). All of these toxins have been linked to changes in behavior, perception, cognition or motor ability. Children who have been exposed to lead, arsenic, aluminum, mercury or cadmium can have permanent neurological damage including attention deficits, emotional and behavioral problems.

Nutrition deficiencies

Nutritional deficiencies have been shown throughout the literature to make a significant impact on the learning and behavior of children. For example, in one study reading skills and IQ tests improved significantly after children started taking multivitamins. Another study showed that learning-disabled children who were placed on vitamin/mineral supplements improved in reading comprehension, their grades improved and those in special education classes were able to become mainstreamed. Those that discontinued the treatment saw their skills drop off, and those who remained on the therapy continued to improve. Research continues to show that poor nutritional habits in children lead to low concentrations of water-soluble vitamins in the blood, impair brain function and subsequently cause violence and other serious antisocial behavior. After correcting the nutrient intake, either by a well-balanced diet or low-dose vitamin/mineral supplementation, this corrected the low concentrations of vitamins in the blood, improved brain function and subsequently lowered institutional violence and antisocial behavior by almost half. The brain and the rest of the body need nutrients for normal vital functioning. Therefore, brain function can be affected by any nutrient deficiency or imbalance. ADHD children often have nutrition deficiencies or imbalances that if corrected can make a significant impact on their behavior.

> *Dietary influences . . . have been linked to hyperactivity.*

Zinc deficiency has been noted in children with ADHD. Hyperactive children had significantly lower zinc levels in hair, blood, fingernail and urine compared to the age and sex-matched controls. The yellow food dye tartrazine may bind to zinc in the blood as a chelating agent and reduce levels of zinc in the blood. Another study found that ADHD children with zinc deficiency had a poorer response to amphetamine treatment.

Magnesium was linked with ADHD in a study involving ADHD children with a recognized magnesium deficiency in the blood. In a period of six months, those examined regularly took magnesium preparations in a dose of approximately 200 mg/day. After a period of six months, there was an increase in magnesium content in hair and a significant decrease of hyperactivity compared to their clinical state before the supplementation and the control group, which was not treated with magnesium.

Vitamin B6 (pyridoxine) is an essential component in a majority of the metabolic pathways of amino acids, including decarboxylation pathways for dopamine, adrenaline and serotonin. One study reported that B vitamins improved the behavior of some children with ADHD in comparison to methylphenidate. In addition, it was further investigated giving children who were responsive to methylphenidate, supplementation of B6. In a double blind, multiple crossover trial, each child received placebo, low and high doses of methylphenidate, and low and high doses of B6 in a 21-week period. Results showed that serotonin blood levels increased dramatically on B6, and teacher ratings showed a 90% level of statistical trend in favor of B6 being slightly more effective than methylphenidate.

> *Chinese herbal therapies have been used in numerous studies with children who had ADHD and proved to be very effective.*

There is an abundance of information correlating the connection of ADHD and essential fatty acids (EFA). There are two main classes of fatty acids—omega-3 and omega-6. C22:6 omega-3 (docosahexaenoic acid, DHA) and C20:4 omega-6 (arachidonic acid) are in human breast milk. Unfortunately, the average DHA content of breast milk in the US is the lowest in the world; probably due to the fact Americans eat comparatively little fish. DHA is the building block of human brain tissue and is abundant in the gray matter of the brain and in the retina. Low levels of DHA have been associated with depression, memory loss, dementia, and visual problems. Low DHA levels have been linked to low brain serotonin levels, which can be connected to depression, suicide and violence. Researchers at Purdue University found that subclinical deficiency in DHA is responsible for the abnormal behavior of children with ADHD. They pointed out the supplementation with a long-chain omega-6 fatty acid (evening primrose oil) was unsuccessful in ameliorating ADHD and this is believed to be due to ADHD children needing more omega-3 fatty acids than more omega-6 acids. The researchers also found that children with ADHD were less often breastfed as infants than were children without ADHD. Breast milk is an excellent source of DHA. . . .

Proanthocyanidins may prove effective in treating ADHD. It was reported in a pediatric practice that children were treated with nutritional supplements similar to pycnogenol (pine bark extract). The biologically active compounds found in pycnogenol are oligomeric proanthocyanidins (OPCs). The results showed that patients in areas relating to sustained attention and distractibility, rather than hyperactivity and impulsivity found the most significant improvement. A few side effects were noted in some children becoming irritable and having decreased energy. OPCs are a class of flavonoids. Flavonoids are a group of polyphenolic substances, which are present in most plants. OPCs have been extracted from many plants including apples, berries, grapes, raspberries and may also be present in many red wines.

Alternative therapies

When treating ADHD, homeopathy should be considered as a treatment option. In a study comparing the effectiveness of homeopathy vs. methylphenidate it was found that in cases where treatment of the hyperactive child was not immediate, homeopathy is a valuable alternative to methylphenidate. The reported results of the homeopathic treatment appear to the similar to the effects of methylphenidate. Only in children who did not achieve the high level of sensory integration for school had to be changed to methylphenidate. In preschoolers, homeopathy appears to be particularly useful in the treatment of ADHD.

> *Alternative therapies should be considered as viable options to Ritalin.*

Chinese herbal therapies have been used in numerous studies with children who had ADHD and proved to be very effective. From a traditional Chinese medical viewpoint, ADD is caused by a "kidney essence deficiency" that affects brain development. Furthermore, the yin aspect of the kidney is mainly deficient, which leads to excessive statement of yang. This excessive yang can manifest as hyperactivity and wandering of the mind. Therefore ADD should be treated by nourishing the kidney yin, opening the heart orifices (which are the passages that affect the brain function), and settling the agitated yang. The main herbs that can be used for nourishing the kidney in ADD children are rehmannia, tortoise shell, deer antler gelatin, lycium, and cornus. In clearing the heart orifices and enhancing the mental function the main herbs used are scorus, polygala, curcuma, and alpinia. To settle an agitated yang energy (manifesting as hyperactivity and insomnia) the alleged "heavy sedating agents" are used. The traditional idea is that these mineral-rich substances bear down on the rising and disordered yang. The main substances given for ADD by Chinese doctors are dragon bone or dragon teeth, oyster shell or mother of pearl, succinum, and cinnabar.

One study showing the effectiveness of Chinese herbals on ADHD children used a sugar paste. Two formulas were made in this form—*Zhili Tangjiang*, composed mainly of acorus and polygala, and *Kangyi Tangjiang*, which contained acorus, polygala, plus tortoise shell, hoelen, dragon bone, alpinia, dioscorea, and lotus seeds. The dose of these pastes was 10–15 ml each time, two to three times per day. Of 170 cases (two studies), 132 (77%) were improved. Treatment time was approximately one month. Another study showed 30 children with ADD were treated with a syrup and powder, for two to four months, with the result that 22 (73%) showed improvements. The syrup was made with alpinia, hoshou-wu, lycium, dragon bone, oyster shell, acorus, curcuma, and salvia, boiled down to a thick liquid and preserved with benzoic acid. Three times per day, the children would take 25 ml of the liquid and 2 grams of deer antler powder. A similar method was used in a study of 50 children with ADD who consumed a decoction of acorus, polygala, dragon bone, and oyster shell, modified by adding three to six herbs according to symptoms, and who also consumed a powder of succinum. The duration of the therapy was not specified but 38 of the children (76%) showed improvements. . . .

This paper discusses some of the alternative options for treating attention deficit hyperactivity disorder in children. This has become a serious condition that is affecting many children today. Ritalin, the most popular pharmaceutical choice in treating ADHD, has many short- and long-term side effects. Alternative therapies should be considered as viable options to Ritalin. There are many effective alternative treatments that can be used to treat and manage ADHD.

Organizations to Contact

The editors have compiled the following list of organizations concerned with the issues debated in this book. The descriptions are derived from materials provided by the organizations. All have publications or information available for interested readers. The list was compiled on the date of publication of the present volume; names, addresses, phone and fax numbers, and e-mail and Internet addresses may change. Be aware that many organizations take several weeks or longer to respond to inquiries, so allow as much time as possible.

ADD Action Group
PO Box 1440, Ansonia Station, New York, NY 10023
(212) 769-2457
Web site: www.addgroup.org

The ADD Action Group is a nonprofit organization that works to find alternative solutions for attention deficit disorder and other learning disablties. It believes that ADD has more than one cause and that different individuals require differing solutions. It produces educational videotapes and carries articles and resources on its Web site.

American Academy of Child and Adolescent Psychiatry (AACAP)
3615 Wisconsin Ave. NW, Washington, DC 20016-3007
(202) 966-7300 • fax: (202) 966-2891
Web site: www.aacap.org

AACAP is a nonprofit organization that supports and advances child and adolescent psychiatry through research and the distribution of information. The academy's goal is to provide information that will remove the stigma associated with mental illnesses and assure proper treatment for children who suffer from mental or behavioral disorders. It publishes the monthly *Journal of the American Academy of Child and Adolescent Psychiatry* and the fact sheets "Children Who Can't Pay Attention/ADHD" and "Psychiatric Medications for Children and Adolescents: Questions to Ask."

American Academy of Pediatrics (AAP)
141 Northwest Point Blvd., Elk Grove Village, IL 60007-1098
(847) 434-4000 • fax: (847) 434-8000
Web site: www.aap.org

AAP is a professional member organization of pediatricians in the United States, Canada, and Latin America who work together to address the health needs of children. It has developed the books *ADHD: A Complete and Authoritative Guide* and *Understanding ADHD* based on its clinical practice guidelines. Its Web site also includes articles and audio files with information on the disorder.

American Psychiatric Association (APA)
1000 Wilson Blvd., Suite 1825, Arlington, VA 22209
(703) 907-7300
e-mail: apa@psych.org • Web site: www.psych.org

An organization of psychiatrists dedicated to studying the nature, treatment, and prevention of mental disorders, the APA helps create mental health policies, distributes information about psychiatry, and promotes psychiatric research and education. It publishes the *American Journal of Psychiatry* monthly and fact sheets on mental disorders, including ADHD.

American Psychological Association (APA)
750 First St. NE, Washington, DC 20002-4242
(202) 336-5500 • fax: (202) 336-5708
e-mail: public.affairs@apa.org • Web site: www.apa.org

The American Psychological Association is the largest scientific and professional organization representing psychology in the United States and is the world's largest association of psychologists. It publishes numerous books, including *Parenting Children with ADHD: Lessons That Medicine Cannot Teach.* Its Web site includes articles and congressional testimony on ADHD.

Attention Deficit Disorder Association (ADDA)
PO Box 543, Pottsdown, PA 19464
(484) 945-2101 • fax: (610) 970-7520
e-mail: mail@add.org • Web site: www.add.org

ADDA is a national nonprofit organization whose mission is to provide information, resources, and networking to adults with ADHD and professionals working with them. It produces *Focus*, a quarterly journal, and provides information and links about ADHD on its Web site.

Center for the Advancement of Children's Mental Health
1051 Riverside Dr., Unit 78, New York, NY 10032
(212) 543-5334 • fax: (212) 543-5260
Web site: www.kidsmentalhealth.org

The center was established by Columbia University in New York to improve methods of assessing and treating children's mental disorders and to provide up-to-date information to the medical community about ADHD and other pediatric disorders. It publishes the newsletter *Putting Science to Work* and provides information about ADHD on its Web site.

Children and Adults with Attention-Deficit/Hyperactivity Disorder (CHADD)
8181 Professional Pl., Suite 150, Landover, MD 20785
(800) 233-4050 • (301) 306-7070 • fax: (301) 306-7090
e-mail: national@chadd.org • Web site: www.chadd.org

CHADD is a nonprofit organization founded by a group of concerned parents that work to improve the lives of children and adults with attention deficit/hyperactivity disorder through education, advocacy, and support. It publishes the quarterly *Attention!* magazine, books, and many fact sheets about the disorder.

Eagle Forum
PO Box 618, Alton, IL 62002
(618) 462-5415 • fax: (618) 462-8909
e-mail: eagle@eagleforum.org • Web site: www.eagleforum.org

The Eagle Forum is an educational and political organization that advocates traditional family values. It has criticized the use of Ritalin in treating attention deficit/hyperactivity disorder. The organization offers several books and publishes the monthly newsletter *Education Reporter.*

National Center for Gender Issues and AD/HD (NCGI)
3268 Arcadia Pl. NW, Washington, DC 20015
(888) 238-8588 • fax: (207) 244-9933
e-mail: contact@ncgiadd.org • Web site: www.ncgiadd.org

The NCGI works to promote awareness, advocacy, and research on ADHD in women and girls. It produces *ADDvance Online,* a monthly electronic newsletter with information on ADHD.

National Institute of Mental Health (NIMH)
6001 Executive Blvd., Room 8184, MSC 9663, Bethesda, MD 20892-9663
(301) 443-4513 • fax: (301) 443-4279
e-mail: nimhinfo@nih.gov • Web site: www.nimh.nih.gov

NIMH is the federal agency concerned with mental health research. It plans and conducts a comprehensive program of research relating to the causes, prevention, diagnosis, and treatment of mental illnesses. It produces various informational publications on mental disorders and their treatment, including the booklet *Attention Deficit Hyperactivity Disorder.*

Web Sites

Additudemag.com
www.additudemag.com

This companion Web site to the bimonthly *ADDitude Magazine* features online articles and fact sheets on ADHD; readers can also order subscriptions to and back issues of the magazine.

Adhdfraud.org
www.adhdfraud.org

The Web site of neurologist and ADHD critic Fred A. Baughman Jr. containing articles questioning whether ADHD is a real disease.

AdhdNews.com
www.adhdnews.com

AdhdNews.com is an online community where parents of children with ADHD share their experiences. The Web site also includes articles about the disorder and links to other sites.

Focus on ADHD
www.focusonadhd.com

This Web site is an information source designed to educate people about ADHD diagnosis, management, and treatment options. It is produced by McNeil Consumer & Specialty Pharmaceuticals, the manufacturer of Concerta, an ADHD medication.

One A.D.D. Place
www.oneaddplace.com

A "virtual neighborhood" that provides information and resources relating to attention deficit disorder.

Bibliography

Books

Daniel G. Amen — *Healing ADD.* New York: Berkley Books, 2002.

Thomas Armstrong — *The Myth of the A.D.D. Child: 50 Ways to Improve Your Child's Behavior and Attention Span Without Drugs, Labels, or Coercion.* New York: Plume, 1997.

Peter Breggin — *The Ritalin Fact Book: What Your Doctor Won't Tell You About ADHD and Stimulant Drugs.* Cambridge, MA: Perseus Books, 2002.

Richard DeGrandpre — *Ritalin Nation: Rapid-Fire Culture and the Transformation of the Human Consciousness.* New York: W.W. Norton, 1999.

Chris A. Zeigler Dendy and Alex Zeigler — *A Bird's Eye View of Life with ADD and ADHD: Advice from Young Survivors.* Cedar Bluff, AL: Cherish the Children, 2003.

Lawrence H. Diller — *Running on Ritalin: A Physician Reflects on Children, Society, and Performance in a Pill.* New York: Bantam, 1998.

Vidha Bhushan Gupta — *No Apologies for Ritalin.* Oradell, NJ: EP Press, 2000.

Julian Stuart Haber — *ADHD: The Great Misdiagnosis.* Dallas, TX: Taylor, 2000.

George Halasz et al. — *Cries Unheard: A New Look at Attention Deficit Hyperactivity Disorder.* Victoria, Australia: Common Ground, 2003.

Thom Hartmann — *The Edison Gene: ADHD and the Gift of the Hunter Child.* Rochester, VT: Park Street Press, 2003.

Robert W. Hill — *Getting Rid of Ritalin: How Neurofeedback Can Successfully Treat Attention Deficit Disorder Without Drugs.* Charlottesville, VA: Hampton Roads, 2002.

Robert Jergen — *The Little Monster: Growing Up with ADHD.* Lanham, MD: Scarecrow, 2004.

Geoffrey Kewley — *ADHD: Recognition, Reality and Resolution.* Melbourne, Australia: ACER Press, 2001.

Claudia Malacrida — *Cold Comfort: Mothers, Professionals, and Attention Deficit Disorder.* Toronto: University of Toronto Press, 2003.

Kathleen G. Nadeau and Patricia O. Quinn, eds. — *Understanding Women with AD/HD*. Silver Spring, MD: Advantage Books, 2002.

Betty B. Osman — *Learning Disabilities and ADHD: A Family Guide to Living and Learning Together*. New York: John Wiley & Sons, 1997.

Judith Peacock — *ADD and ADHD*. Mankato, MN: LifeMatters, 2002.

Benjamin Polis — *Only a Mother Could Love Him: Attention Deficit Disorder*. New York: Ballantine Books, 2004.

Michael I. Reiff with Sherril Tippins — *ADHD: A Complete and Authoritative Guide for Parents*. Elk Grove Village, IL: American Academy of Pediatrics, 2004.

William Sears and Lynda Thompson — *The A.D.D. Book*. Boston: Little, Brown, 1998.

Alvin Silverstein et al. — *Attention Deficit Disorder*. New York: Franklin Watts, 2001.

Sari Solden — *Journeys Through ADDulthood*. New York: Walker & Company, 2002.

Amy E. Stein — *Fragments: Coping with Attention Deficit Disorder*. New York: Haworth, 2002.

David B. Stein — *Unraveling the ADD/ADHD Fiasco: Successful Parenting Without Drugs*. Kansas City, MO: Andrews McMeel, 2001.

Warren Umansky and Barbara Steinberg Smalley — *AD/HD: Helping Your Child*. New York: Warner Books, 2003.

Sydney Walker — *The Hyperactivity Hoax*. New York: St. Martin's, 1998.

Paul H. Wender — *ADHD: Attention-Deficit Hyperactivity Disorder in Children and Adults*. New York: Oxford University Press, 2000.

Marcia Zimmerman — *The ADD Nutrition Solution: A Drug-Free Thirty-Day Plan*. New York: Holt, 1999.

Periodicals

Daniel G. Amen — "Attention, Doctors: What We Call Attention-Deficit Disorder Is Actually Six Different Conditions. And One-Drug-Fits-All Therapy Isn't Right for Any of Them," *Newsweek*, February 26, 2001.

American Family Physician — "What Is ADHD?" September 1, 2001.

B. Bower — "Cerebral Clues Emerge for Attention Disorder," *Science News*, November 29, 2003.

Kathryn Brown	"New Attention to ADHD Genes: Researchers Are Trying to Tease Apart the Genetic and Environmental Contributions to Childhood's Most Common Mental Disorder," *Science*, July 11, 2003.
Jessi Castro	"I Am a Different Person," *Time*, November 3, 2003.
Dimitri A. Christakis et al.	"Early Television Exposure and Subsequent Attentional Problems in Children," *Pediatrics*, April 2004.
Craig L. Donnelly	"ADHD Medications: Past and Future," *Behavioral Health Management*, May/June 2002.
Harlan R. Gephardt	"Where We Are, and How Well Can We Succeed, at Treating ADHD," *Contemporary Pediatrics*, December 2003.
Malcolm Gladwell	"Running from Ritalin," *New Yorker*, February 15, 1999.
William Norman Grigg	"Ending the Nightmare," *New American*, August 25, 2003.
Bernadine Healy	"The Temperamental Mind," *U.S. News & World Report*, April 26, 2004.
Marisa Hoheb	"Brain Burn," *Scholastic Choices*, February/March 2004.
Beth Kaplanek	"Household Havoc: One Mother's Quest for Quiet on the Home Front," *Psychology Today*, September/October 2002.
Medical Economics	"Many Options for Treating ADHD," March 19, 2004.
Mental Health Weekly	"TV Viewing May Increase Risk of Attention Problems," April 26, 2004.
Paula Moyer	"Curing ADHD: Willpower or Meds?" *Psychology Today*, March/April 2003.
Newsweek	"New Options for ADHD," September 22, 2003.
Kelly Patricia O'Meara	"In ADHD Studies, Pictures May Lie; Researchers Contend That Brain-Imaging Studies Relied on by Doctors for the Last 20 Years to Diagnose Attention-Deficit/Hyperactivity Disorder Are Based on False Data," *Insight on the News*, August 19, 2003.
Kelly Patricia O'Meara	"Putting Power Back in Parental Hands," *Insight on the News*, May 13, 2003.
San Francisco Chronicle	"As Prozac Fades, Strattera Soars," December 29, 2003.
Michael F. Shaughnessy et al.	"An Interview with Lawrence Greenberg About Attention Deficit and Hyperactivity," *Clearing House*, September/October 1999.

Aliya Sternstein	"Unquiet Minds," *Forbes*, November 10, 2003.
Marianne Szegedy-Maszak	"Driven to Distraction," *U.S. News & World Report*, April 26, 2004.
Marianne Szegedy-Maszak	"Tuneups for Misfiring Neurons," *U.S. News & World Report*, April 26, 2004.
Laurie Tarkan	"Attention Disorder Advice, by One Who Knows," *New York Times*, August 26, 2003.
USA Today	"Helping Kids Cope with Impulse Problems," October 2002.
U.S. News & World Report	"Does America Have ADD?" March 26, 2001.
Timothy E. Wilens et al.	"Does Stimulant Therapy of Attention-Deficit/ Hyperactivity Disorder Beget Later Substance Abuse? A Meta-Analytic Review of the Literature," *Pediatrics*, January 2003.

Index

abnormal behavior. *See* behavior, problems with
ABT418, 46
accidents, prone to, 20
Acters Profile for Boys, 78
adaptability, 20
Adderall, 84, 87
addiction. *See* substance abuse
additives, food, 89–90
adolescents, 18, 50
  see also twelve-year-olds
adoption, 44, 50, 87
adrenal glands, 86–87
adrenaline, 92
adults, 9, 11, 88
  with ADHD, 18, 50, 63, 67–70, 87
aggression, 21, 75, 89
  see also anger; violence
agitation, 19
  see also fidgeting; restlessness
air traffic controllers, 68
alcohol, 88
alcoholism, 50
alleles, 44–46
allergies, 50, 86, 89–90
alternative medicine, 86–94
amino acids, 86, 89, 92
amphetamine, 37–38, 88–89, 91
anger, 14, 83–84, 87–88
antisocial behavior. *See* behavior, problems with
anxiety, 26, 30
appetite, loss of, 27, 77, 88
  see also weight, loss of
asthma, 24, 50
atrophy, brain, 30–31
  see also brain, abnormalities in
attention deficit disorder (ADD), 48–51
  see also attention deficit/hyperactivity disorder
attention deficit/hyperactivity disorder (ADHD)
  is a disorder, 9, 11–22, 33–47
    con, 10, 23–32, 63–71
  heredity causes, 10, 43–47, 58–62, 87
    con, 48–51
  television viewing causes, 52–55
    con, 56–62
attention spans, short, 49, 52, 54–55,
60, 74, 93
  see also inattentiveness
Australia, 22

babies, hypersensitive, 49–50
Barr, Cathy L., 44
Baughman, Fred A., Jr., 28
behavior
  modification of, 36–37, 51
  normal, 23–24
  problems with, 10–21, 52–54, 57, 87, 89–92
Behavior Problems Index, 53–54
Beneda, Deena, 86
bipolar disorder, 26, 28, 45
boredom impairment, 68
boys, 35–36, 42, 78, 87
brain
  abnormalities in, 10, 18–20, 30–31, 90–91
  development of, 45, 48–55, 59, 62, 88–89, 92–94
breast feeding, 92
Brown University Child and Adolescent Behavior Newsletter, 43
Bush, Neil, 76–77

caffeine, 88
Canada, 22
careers, 68–70
caregiving, skills of, 49
  see also mother-infant relationship; parents
Carroll, Kyle, 77–78
Carroll, Michael and Jill, 77–78
case studies, 12–15, 23–27, 72–80
Castellanos, F. Xavier, 43
caudate nucleus, 18
causes, 10, 26, 43–51, 58–60, 89–93
Chalice and the Blade, The (Eisler), 66
chemical disorders, 28–29
Chinese herbal therapies, 93–94
cholinergic pathways, 46
Christakis, Dimitri A., 57–59
Clonidine, 84
cloning, positional, 46
clumsiness, 20
cocaine, 33, 37–38, 76, 78, 88
codeine, 76
cognition, social, 20
colic, 14, 50

103